What Experts Are Sayi

CH00669955

"I've encountered a lot of coaches around the world during my journeys. Lee is the most knowledgeable and passionate that I've met. I've seen him implement the lessons in this book to turn a team around first hand. If you're looking to give your team an edge, this is the book to pick up!"

—Chris Kibui, founder of HockeyTutorial

"WIN is like sitting down and having a conversation with Lee. It provides the kind of insight that can only come from one's personal experiences with success and it is as genuine as it gets. If you want to take your life to the next level, this is a great first step on that road."

—Ray Carsillo, Reviews & Previews Editor, former ESPN Radio producer, personality

"I've played for several coaches over my playing career. The ones that have found success all understood the concepts written in this book."

—Bryce Salvador, former NHL Captain (New Jersey Devils) and Player (New Jersey and St. Louis)

"Morale is born of loyalty, patriotism, discipline, and efficiency, all of which breed confidence in self and in comrades. . . .

Morale is at one and the same time the strongest, and the most delicate of growths.

It withstands shocks, even disasters of the battlefield, but can be destroyed utterly by favoritism, neglect, or injustice."

– Dwight D. Eisenhower

CONTENTS

ON WINNING

Did you know that champagne stings your eyes? I love watching athletes and coaches discover this for the first time. One of my favorite photos, currently hanging on my office wall, captures this experience memorably.

In the photo, our captain is holding up a championship trophy just presented to him by the league president. He is surrounded by his teammates and a mist of champagne. His eyes are closed and although it is just a photo, you can still hear his victorious shout. In the same photo, just inches away from this iconic image of victory is one of hilarity. One of our younger players is standing with his mouth open, accidentally spraying nearly a full bottle of champagne up his nose and into his face. Every time I pass that picture, I smile and chuckle at the memory of both the sting (I felt it too that day) and surprise that crossed his face as the alcohol met his eyes. Of course, the distinct burn caused by this tradition is just a small part of the victory celebration.

After spending the next thirty minutes celebrating on the ice together and with our families, both the players and coaches returned to our locker room. It would be the last time this team would be fully together.

After some endearing comments from the head coach and some more celebrating, one of the players shouted to "play the video!" Prior to each playoff game during this postseason, we had a pregame video created to both motivate and focus the players. The theme was "I am a champion," a phrase that was repeated fifteen times in each viewing. When we played the video before games, the players would watch with intense eyes as they let the competitive emotions created by the footage, music, and voice-over flood their hearts with motivation. This postgame showing had a very different feel. With smiles on their faces and drinks in their hands, every single member of the team shouted, "I AM A CHAMPION!" during each spot in the video. It was a surreal moment that perfectly exhibited the accomplishment of a communal goal, but more importantly it showed how close this group had become over the grueling eight-month hockey season.

During that season while I served as a player development coach, my team overcame incredible odds to surprise everyone and win the league's playoff championship. In the prior season, the team finished second to last and did not make the playoffs—and early expectations were that they would finish near the same spot in the current season. Yet here they were, celebrating, hugging, and shouting until their voices were gone while sharing what will be remembered as one of the greatest moments in their lives.

The entire experience begged the question: What did this team do differently to break through and become champions in such a short time? It wasn't superior talent, as the team had no players named to the First All-Star Team after the season. It wasn't better endurance, as the team had fewer practices than any of its competitors. It wasn't money, as the team had one of the lowest payrolls and budgets in the league. What was it?

The answer is simple. This team developed a *connection* that enabled them to work better together than every other team. From the head coach who was a brilliant tactician, to the players who all had a common will to work and win, to the staff who dedicated countless hours to the team, this group shared a special bond that carried them to a championship together.

YOU CAN START WINNING, RIGHT NOW

Depending on where you sit within your organization, "winning" can be defined in many ways. For some, winning is defined by championships, while others focus on just the next game. If you are part of a team's coaching staff, winning may encompass watching athletes reach the next level of their potential. If you work on the business end of an organization, winning may be defined by revenue generated or fan attendance. No matter how you define it, your goal is to get there as fast and efficiently as possible.

Of course, winning isn't easy—if it were, everyone would do it. The truth is that each season, only one team can ultimately win the championship. My goal with this book is to give you the tools—and define the winning elements—to help you be that team, now and into the future.

In business, that ultimate goal you choose is similar to winning a championship as a sports team. It's a full-season campaign and the principles are very similar.

Finding the Winning Edge

For most coaches and managers, finding the "edge" needed to create a championship team is a multifaceted effort. First priority for most organizations is to secure the best athletic talent possible within their means. No doubt, your athletes' abilities on the chosen field of play are critical to the team's successful execution.

Beyond talent, the head coach and staff must provide inspired leadership along with strong leaders from within the player population. While responsibilities within the coaching staff and team roster may be spread out or centralized—depending on the team—as the coach, your ability to lead and perhaps more importantly, your team's willingness to be led contribute significantly to the successful outcome.

An ability to understand (and in some cases the ability to create) the tactics of your chosen sport is also often cited as an essential ingredient for the winning team. Getting "out-coached" is a common line from both media and fans, when two tacticians go head-to-head in a sports contest. Make no mistake: in spite of talent and leadership, sometimes the right tactical decisions can win or lose a game.

Aside from talent, leadership, and tactics, the intangible contributions of any sports team such as overall health of players—ranging from dodging illness to avoiding injury— also affect the bottom line. Perhaps the most elusive element is timing; sometimes your team hits losing streaks when it seems they are working harder than ever, and other times your team floats into winning streaks where exceptional play may seem to come out of nowhere.

Many teams base their overall team strategies, which can encompass everything from management style down to the actual plays the team will use, on those of the previous year's champion. Some coaches focus on making sure their team has the most sophisticated, state-of-the-art equipment, hoping that will give their athletes extra leverage. Some coaches try to adopt the tactics (whether that be overall Xs and Os on the coach's board or utilizing specific positions in a certain way) that proved successful for top teams in the previous season. The quest to find the ingredient that will propel your team into the lead and champion-ship "promised land" is an always-evolving endeavor in the world of coaching.

All of these elements are essential to a team's success, but they will not produce the complete championship package. Having the best talent does not guarantee the right chem-istry in a sports team any more than having great leaders guarantees motivation in the locker room. Moreover, your team can have the best tactician in your sport, but if those tactics are not communicated properly to your players, that asset is useless. While you have very little control over ill-ness and injury, if your team is not mentally prepared to face the adversity that comes with a sports season, it can be catastrophic for your campaign.

In order to win, your team, your staff, and all the requisite skills and strategies must be synchronized in excellence—but there is another, often-overlooked yet essential ingredi-ent that must be present to find success. It is something all championship teams share—something so sacred in sports it is rarely discussed: the creation, nurturing, and mainte-nance of a *total team bond*.

THE BOND

It was on a brisk fall afternoon during my freshman year of college that twenty of my teammates and I found ourselves crawling through goose shit. The cold football field we were trekking across on our hands and knees was adjacent to the ice rink we would call home that season. A rainstorm the night before had turned the field into a freezing soup of grass, mud, and the fertilizer the Canadian geese left behind. Needless to say, all of us would rather have been on the ice—yet there we were, ruining our clothes and getting covered in greenish-black slime.

While we pushed through the filth, we heard a booming voice over our shoulders. "GET TO THE LINE! DO NOT STOP MOVING UNTIL YOU GET TO THE LINE." We dared not look back at the man screaming, for fear of being singled out.

We grunted and groaned as every movement we made forward sucked us farther into the muck. Yet steadily we pressed on.

"I have to stop." I looked to my right to see one of my teammates looking at me. He was skinny for a hockey player, and the exercise was clearly taking a toll on him.

"Don't stop. Whatever you do, don't stop," I said between breaths. He drove his arm forward one more time and then put his forehead down right into the mud. He just didn't have any more. I signaled over him to my teammate to his right. "Grab his right arm and I'll grab the left!" Without thinking, we grabbed hold of our teammate and started to drag him to the line with us. I feared that any second the voice would be over my shoulder yelling at me to let him go, but it never came. After a few more minutes of pain and struggle, we crossed the 50-yard line of the field (we started at the goal line). Exhausted and spattered with crap, we flipped over to catch our breath. The nearby geese on the field gave us a quizzical look, their loud squawking resembling more of a maniacal laugh than an objection to us plowing through their territory.

While we stared up at the gray sky, a US marine came into our field of view and stood hovering over us. In our fatigued state, his six-foot-two-inch stature looking down at us was a menacing sight. He didn't say anything, but he had an evil smirk on his face. As he walked away, he shouted for us to get into push-up position. Although our arms were exhausted from the crawl, we flipped over and did it without question. The drudgery continued . . .

Throughout the season at select times, the marine would come back and run us through similar drills. Our coach had brought this servant of our country on board to teach discipline and bring the players together. As the year went on, he became more and more cordial with us, although the workout intensity stayed the same. We didn't know it at the time, but these "group bonding" sessions were going to play a big part in our exhilarating and ultimately successful championship season.

These off-ice training gatherings created a mutual understanding and belief that we could go through anything together—including goose shit. It also gave us an edge on the opposition, all season long. We were not the most talented team or the most experienced; in fact, we had the largest freshman class in our division. However, we often outworked our opponents, and when we would lose a game, we came back even harder and more aggressively the following match. When the playoffs began, the opposition didn't stand a chance against our "team first" philosophy.

While winning that championship was one of many highlights from my playing career, the lessons I learned from my time on that filthy field would become the foundation of my coaching philosophy. At the end of every group session, we heard this chant: "Team. Teammates. Self. That is how we prioritize within this club." The phrase, which borrows heavily from the Navy SEAL code, still resonates with me today.

When joining the military, regardless of the branch and in most cases regardless of country, all recruits must go through some form of basic training, also known as "boot camp." These programs exist to test the recruits' physical and mental abilities before they are accepted as a soldier, airman, seaman, or marine in the armed forces.

It's a process of discovering weaknesses and bringing out the best in each person for the mission. Through humility and hard work, recruits are expected to push past their comfort zone and discover new levels of ability. At the same time, individuals are taught the importance and power that comes with putting the team's needs ahead of their own. Those that cannot meet these requirements are dropped from the program. Those that pass become part of the bravest and most unified teams on earth.

When it comes to building a sports team, although the overall mission differs from the military, the goals are the same—to create a group of people that will work together to achieve victory.

The military and athletic teams are similar in many ways; both wear uniforms, have leadership figures, and represent a community, educational institution, or country. These are all common aspects of what makes a team. What makes them winners is the ability to maintain a community of trust, clear laws of communication, individual and group account-ability, and the ability to face adversity as a group. Above all, at the core of both sports teams and military institutions is an unwavering respect and understanding for maintaining and believing in the team bond. Only when that exists will victory consistently be yours.

WHAT IS "THE BOND"?

Think about every great team you've ever been part of as a teammate or coach. In most if not all circumstances, moti-vation to win came from your belief in each other—not just a belief in yourself. You were able to dig deep and find the will to run a little faster and drive a little harder. That bond created a fire inside of you and your teammates that was so intense, no one outside of your group could penetrate it. This was your family, your home, and your sanctuary away from real life. You sweated, bled, and won for each other.

Establishing a team bond is the consummate starting point for any team whose goal is to win a championship.

Reach back and feel the incredible power that you all felt to-gether in victory. Remember how, in the moment when you triumphed as a group and won, anything seemed possible. As a coach, imagine the power you would have if you could re-create this for your team and duplicate it year after year with remarkable consistency. Because if you truly believe, if you know the group you have developed has that trust in each other and "has your back," together you can learn, grow, and go against adversity in any form, and you will be unstoppable.

Common goals are what make a team. A true team bond is the fuel that drives a team to accomplish those goals and achieve greatness. It's the glue that holds everything together.

No matter where you are in the process of becoming a successful team—whether it's "so close you can taste it," or if it seems "a million miles away"—establishing a true team bond is the foundation that produces both immediate and lasting results.

A bonded team will beat a group of individuals, even when those individuals have more talent. I believe in this to my core, and I have experienced it and seen it work time and time again.

Many coaches believe that the team bond occurs naturally in sport. Team bonds come easier to some teams than others, but it is never something that happens automatically. Successful bonds must be actively developed and then nurtured throughout the course of a season. The process requires you to be in touch with your team's emotions (both as a group and individuals), to be creative in the ways you motivate and inspire your squad, and perhaps hardest of all, to be patient in the face of massive adversity.

The process for developing this foundation starts long before players arrive for their first day of practice or training camp. And it doesn't stop until the final game is over. Building a bond requires you and your players to establish a shared understanding of several ideals. Words like trust, accountability, leadership, and adversity all need to be clearly defined and understood. A communication structure—that runs from the head coach to the coaching staff, through the captains to the players, and back the other way—must be created. It is critically important to recognize and neutralize threats or cancers that can weaken and kill your team bond.

The existence and understanding of these ideals is just a starting point. Throughout the season you will need to work with your team and staff to harness each aspect, while also conducting your squad to work in harmony. When this is achieved, winning will be possible.

A sports season is a living thing. Just like life, it can have ups, downs, twists, and turns.

No matter how long you have been coaching or a player has been active—and though there will be plenty of repetition and routine—no two days in sports are ever the same. Your ability to prepare your team to face the grind together is the ultimate foundation for finding success.

Just prior to starting his political career in 1881, Theodore Roosevelt said, "It is not often that a man can make opportunities for himself. But he can put himself in such shape that when or if the opportunities come, he is ready." That mindset took Teddy all the way to the White House. Establishing that thinking through a team bond will enable your players to see opportunity everywhere and take you all to a championship.

TRUST 2

When you hear the word *trust*, what thoughts come to mind?

You trust the postal service will deliver your mail. You trust friends not to go behind your back. You trust child-care providers or family members to watch your children. You trust a carefully selected group of individuals with your life. Clearly, there are many different levels of trust.

When you think about it, trust may be the most sacred emotional element of our lives. If someone breaks your trust, how hard is it for him or her to earn it back? Even if they manage to reclaim a small portion, you may never be able to fully trust that person again.

Trust is the basis for all relationships. It is the keystone on which we build and expand our experiences with others. Without trust, growth would not be possible. This is why trust must be the foundation of your team bond. Simply put, trust needs to be a sacred and unbreakable commitment agreed to, both inside and outside the locker room, by every member.

We are all raised differently and in a variety of environments where the definition of trust can differ drastically. For example, some families are incredibly close, and all members are expected to pull their weight for each other; other families are broken and siblings, parents, and relatives barely talk to each other. When you bring a group of people together, odds are that a common understanding of how trust applies to your sports family does not already exist—so it is up to you as coach to develop one.

> **Trust needs to be a sacred and unbreakable commitment agreed to, both inside and outside the locker room, by every member.**

In my experiences in sports teams, trust is most often broken because the concept of trust and how it applies to the team has not clearly been defined to players and coaches prior to the season.

Think about the fact that we use the word "break" when describing trust. We don't commonly say we *"lose"* trust, or we haven't "*maintained*" trust—we *break* trust when one person or more decides to deceive someone else. In regards to your team, even a small crack in that trust will also result in a crack in your team bond. Trust, or the lack of it, has the power to build or destroy your entire team bond faster than any other element discussed in this book.

In its most rudimentary form, trust is the reliance on the integrity and strength of another person. When we speak about trust, we use words like belief, expectation, faith, and conviction—all words and concepts we have heard in locker-room speeches throughout our lives.

The enemy of trust—distrust—is defined as regarding someone with doubt or suspicion. When discussing distrust, we use words like deception, doubt, skepticism, and disbelief. If terms like these are creeping into your locker room, you have a problem.

One of the main goals for your team, in addition to winning, must be to make sure that trust is never broken between anyone inside your locker room. If it is broken, it needs to be quickly restored. If you coach a middle school or high school team, you may need lots of consistent instruction and reinforcement to maintain trust within your team. In order to do this, your coaching staff and players must clearly define and understand why trust is important and how it applies to the team.

Establishing this communal definition for trust is the starting point for your bond. However, even when clearly defined, trust can still be vulnerable to damage. Maintaining and nurturing trust throughout the year is the glue that will keep things together. Creating and implementing a concrete plan for how trust applies to your team is imperative from the start, if you want to win.

THE CIRCLE OF TRUST

As a coach, establishing an internal trust philosophy, a crystal-clear plan for how trust will apply to every player and coach on your team, should be initiated as early as possible in the season. Whether at a training camp or the first team function, invite your players to a meeting with the coaching staff and explain how the concept of trust will apply to your team for the season.

You can introduce trust to your team using a concept called the *circle of trust*. No matter whether your first time with a group is before or during a season, this is something to share during the first meeting or practice you hold. After introductions and brief statements, draw a large circle on a board and write the word "TRUST" in large letters right in the center. In addition to trust, write the words "athletes," "trainers," and "coaches." On the outside of the circle, write "owners," "admin," "staff," "media," and "fans." Once this diagram is in place, explain that you, the coaching staff, and the players live inside this circle of trust. Within this area, you must all commit to trusting each other and more importantly, commit to respecting that trust throughout the entire season. In short, what's said, done, or decided in this circle stays in the circle, just like what is said in the locker room stays in the locker room. The circle of trust represents your team's internal commitment to each other and serves as the beating heart of your team bond.

You might want to explain that trust and respect are two different things. While the ownership, administration, staff, fans, and other groups of people live outside your circle of trust, they still deserve respect. However, no matter how influential these people may be to the actual operations, unless they are an essential part of what happens in the locker room, they must be left outside the circle. The reason for this is to neutralize the potential for players or coaches to influence or be influenced by individuals who may not understand the tactics or goals set by the group as a whole. While everyone may have the best intentions for the team, one seed of doubt or false expectation for the group or an individual can inadvertently turn the ship off course. In short, you want to avoid having too many leaders and not enough team members.

THE COMMUNICATION LADDER AS IT APPLIES TO TRUST AND LEADERSHIP

Forming the circle of trust is the first step to creating an environment for success; the second step is to create an understanding of how communication works in your locker room.

Establishing a clear order of information flow for your room is a map for everyone to follow when issues of trust are on the line. We will go much deeper into communication later in the book, but for now understand that establishing a communication ladder is imperative for maintaining trust in your room. It is similar to the chain of command in the military. In battle, clear and concise communication is imperative to preserve life and achieve objectives. Although the stakes are much higher for the armed forces, the same hierarchical approach promotes efficient communication in sports. Stress the importance of this procedure to your team, your coaches, and everyone who will be part of the team for the season.

A strong understanding of a communication protocol will prevent many common problems before they start. For example, it will deter members of your team from accidentally (or purposely) going behind each other's backs, as well as eliminate the possibility that players will think coaches have placed some players above others.

To be clear, this communication directive is not meant to discourage interaction between players and coaches. In fact, strong communication should be encouraged.

Typically, the ladder starts with the head coach or manager on top, followed by assistant coaches, then captains or elected team leaders, and finishes with the remaining player population. Team trainers, equipment staff, and any other members of your organization who have constant close contact with the team should also be appropriately incorporated into the ladder. While the ladder establishes a hierarchy, communication should still work both ways without taking any shortcuts.

If a player on your team disagrees with a choice the coaching staff has made or how the team is managed in general, they should have the opportunity to bring that complaint to a team captain. In turn, the captain should share it with the coaching staff, if he or she feels it is not something they can handle on their own. This process alleviates any discomfort or hesitancy a player might have about bringing something up directly to the coach, while also allowing them to get any issue off their chest. Without this flow of communication in place, players may start to commiserate within the team, which can grow into a major collective threat to your team bond over time.

Another common example of how useful the order of operations can be is when, inevitably, a player has a problem with another player. Unless the situation is public knowledge to the entire team already (in which case it should be dealt with swiftly), the leaders on your roster should be called on to handle it. If a player goes right to the coach to discuss the problem, it can easily be perceived as going behind a teammate's back. Moreover, if you as the coach take action after only hearing one side of the story, players may assume that you are playing favorites.

As the coach, you have free rein to speak to anyone on the team at any time. However, utilizing the ladder can benefit you as well. As the overall leader of the locker room, your voice is most likely heard more than anyone's. Depending on what message you are trying to send, it may be beneficial to allow someone else on the ladder to relay the message. For example, if you are planning a team function such as a meal or meeting, let your team leaders relay the memo to the team. The message will get across and you will also enable him or her as a leader (thereby strengthening your bond with them).

Another example—perhaps you are trying to motivate a player who has had a rough time but is not very responsive to you. Ask one of your team leaders to approach the player instead. Sometimes the voice of a fellow teammate can have a more dramatic effect than the voice of a coach. Small things like these also keep your players from feeling they are being micromanaged or are under a microscope.

In addition to these examples, members of your team should understand that when troubles occur within the circle of trust, those involved in the situation are not the only ones responsible for taking action. In reality, when glitches occur within your locker room, your entire group must be accountable to each other. Everyone has the responsibility to speak up or take action if they believe a problem has the potential to affect your team bond.

At the end of the day, we are all human beings. Odds are there isn't an evil member of your team who is secretly conspiring to tear it apart. However, mistakes are inevitable and problems will occur no matter how hard you try to keep them from happening. Your team's ability to respond appropriately to these situations relies largely on their willingness to trust each other and to effectively use the communication ladder you have developed.

TRUST IN THE COACH

A popular saying in sports is that "attitude reflects leadership," and there is no greater barometer for that phrase than you. As the coach of your team, you—more than anyone else—are responsible for keeping the torch of trust burning brightly for your group. No one person in your circle of trust has more power to stoke the flame or extin-

> Never compromise the trust you have built with your players for anything.

guish it. It must be understood that while you are at the top of the trust ladder, you are not exempt from it. Never compromise the trust you have built with your players for anything. It's one of the fastest ways to destroy your bond and undermine your team's foundation.

Shortcuts to winning can be very tempting. Like most quick fixes, they may work in the immediate future but in the long run they often do more harm than good. You have likely seen this play out in colleges and middle or high school teams. As student-athletes, players must maintain a certain grade point average (GPA) to remain eligible, and most coaches enforce that rule without question. Unfortunately, for some sports teams, GPA eligibility is checked quarterly and not every week. As a result, on some teams, a player who is failing in school can continue to play through the end of the academic quarter. This brings up a moral dilemma. As the coach, if that player is a star athlete, do you continue to let them play until the term ends?

In pro sports this scenario plays out a bit differently. Just like high school and college, professional coaches establish rules for all players to follow. Sometimes players that find success on the field or court can grow a big head and start to think the rules don't apply to them. This can result in a player having a big mouth outside the arena or making selfish or unorthodox plays during a game. This is a sticky situation for most coaches. Odds are that player is paid well and their ability to perform may directly influence the outcome of a game. Do you bend the rules for this person so you can win?

In all these scenarios, middle/high school, college, and pro, the short-term success you may find from allowing these players to slide will ultimately destroy your team bond. By allowing any one player the chance to bend the rules, you are essentially telling your entire team that you do not respect the guidelines that you created. From your point of view, you may think you are doing what you need to do to win. From the point of view of your players, you are breaking the team trust that *you* built—making you a hypocrite. When that aspect of the bond begins to break down, you will find your athletes begin to give less and less to the team each day. You must ask yourself: Regardless of how much you know about your sport and how impressive your past record is—how can a team follow someone they don't trust completely?

TRUST IN OTHER COACHES

Assistant and associate coaches can be a lot like players. They all want a purpose and the chance to show what they can do for the team. Choosing a trustworthy coaching staff that understands your goals for the team and organization is essential.

Good coaches think they know everything, and great coaches understand that they don't. Beyond that, great coaches know what their own weaknesses are. No matter how strong a coach is at certain aspects of the game, no one is perfect. We all have facets of our approach to coaching that may be lacking or underdeveloped. Your ability to understand your own shortcomings and surround yourself with trustworthy individuals that fill in those gaps is as important as finding the right player for each position on the team. The art of coaching, just like sport, is always evolving. For that reason, it is important to view your coaching staff as more of a think tank than a support group.

Your coaching staff is a micro-team inside the overall group. If you and your staff aren't functioning as an impenetrable coaching team with a unified purpose, how can your athletes emulate the same inside the locker room? Prior to the start of the season, make sure to have numerous meetings with your assistant coaches and other staff members to communicate your management philosophy and communication ladder. Just like players, assistant coaches and auxiliary staff will question their role on a team if it's not clearly defined. Make sure to explain to each person how you see them being involved and what they can bring to the team concept and the overall bond. Allow them to make suggestions and ask questions. Make sure that everyone feels they have a voice, while making sure they respect their place in the overall authority of the team.

Coaches naturally have disagreements and differing opinions on how the team's and individuals' games should be executed. This is because many coaches tend to be students of the game. With that said, we all learn the game differently. You should understand this and strive to create a healthy environment where every coach can bring their knowledge and thoughts to the table, to be utilized to benefit the team. You should welcome the potential differences of perspective—behind closed doors so the conversations can't be overheard or misunderstood—in an open, collaborative environment that encourages multiple ideas along with good communication. This is how learning can take place.

In order to assure that your coaching bond stays as strong as possible, plan weekly meetings with your staff to clarify issues and communicate important details, as well as to discuss upcoming strategies. Don't overcomplicate meetings, but focus on how the staff is operating, in addition to practice and game strategies. Your staff should feel comfortable discussing both positive and negative aspects of the coaching unit as well as team issues. Their opinion needs to matter and be taken seriously.

Above all, make it known that while you encourage conversations and debate amongst staff, disagreements between staff should not be aired in public or where team members can overhear. In the name of professionalism, request that differences of opinion be resolved privately; all efforts should focus on presenting a unified position to the team and the fans. At the end of each day, your and your staff's ability to come across to your players as a cohesive and impenetrable unit will set the ultimate example for them to do the same with their teammates.

IDENTITY 3

In the baseball movie *The Natural,* the New York Knights (a fictional National League baseball team) are lifted out of their division's basement by the play of Roy Hobbs. Portrayed by Robert Redford, Hobbs was on track to become the greatest player of all time before he tragically fell out of baseball at a young age due to an unfortunate accident. After two decades of recovery—and now as a middle-aged rookie—he decides to give playing the game of baseball one last shot with the last-place Knights, while he still has the ability.

In addition to his enduring skill, also complementing Hobbs' game is an almost mythological baseball bat that he created as a child with lumber from a tree that was struck by lightning near his childhood home. Etched into the bat is the nickname "Wonderboy," followed by a lightning bolt. When he finally makes it to the Major Leagues, Hobbs and his bat quickly become lore of the game to media, fans, and even the players on his team. Inspired by Hobbs's incredible and inspirational play, one of his teammates creates a lightning patch—an exact replica of the one on Hobbs' bat—to wear on the arm of his jersey. Almost immediately, he has extra jump in his step and power in his swing. Soon after, the entire team has lightning patches on their baseball uniforms and the team makes an incredible turnaround to go on and win the pennant.

I know this was just a movie, and magical bats and patches are more likely to be categorized as superstition in the eyes of most people. The idea is that a team found an identity that players could rally around. It is a very real concept that can and should be applied to your team.

One does not need to look far for other examples of how a strong identity has helped a team succeed.

In 1980, the US men's Olympic "miracle" hockey team bonded externally because they were Americans taking on the Soviet Union (who housed the greatest hockey team of all time) and internally as they put aside their domestic hockey rivalries to prove themselves to a dictatorial coach. Herb Brooks, the coach, masterfully manipulated his team to bond through a relentless six-month training camp preceding the Olympics, in which the players were subjected to grueling workouts, practices, games, and even a written test. The resulting close-knit team triumphed over the Soviet Union to win an Olympic gold medal and achieved what many regard as the greatest sports moment of the twentieth century.

Identity can encompass many different things in sports. Your team represents the organization you work for—a company, a city, or a school. Your team represents the community and fans who come to watch and support. Your team also represents each other as individuals and as a group and an attitude and style of play. These are all very different types of identity, and they are all important for establishing your team bond.

One of the beautiful things about creating and establishing an identity in sports is that it is almost always unique. In a profession where there is so much routine and repetiveness, identity is the ever-changing denominator that creates new meaning for your team. Having a team identity will give your players a common purpose, in addition to something tangible they can grab on to for motivation when they need a mental boost.

Establishing an identity also helps your players to build an "us versus them" attitude. Having the ability to remind your team at key moments of the season exactly who and what they represent can help to amplify the level of competitiveness (something that should always be welcomed) in the locker room. This gives your team a mental advantage over an opponent who may not have a similar philosophy.

Finding and establishing your team identity is like peeling back the layers of an onion—there are many. When you examine each layer of identity more closely, you will see there are many motivational ideals that are important to creating a "team first" mentality.

ORGANIZATIONAL IDENTITY

Among the many rules that exist within my locker rooms, two specifically maintain the importance of organizational identity:

1. Your jersey is never to touch the floor.

2. You are never to disrespect, deface, or walk on or across a team logo.

Do this to establish the idea that the team colors and crest are not just threads on each player's jersey, but a seal and shield they are privileged to carry as a member of the organization. Make sure your team takes the saying, "The name on the front of the jersey (the team name) means more than the name on the back (individual player's name)" seriously. It is an important statement that communicates the importance of what they represent.

Organizational identity encompasses your players' commitment to representing the organization with class and determination at all times.

Introduce the identity in all its facets to each player, starting with the first day they officially become part of your team. Team identity includes the team's organizational history, attitude, and past champions or record holders. Use a variety of approaches to communicate this unique identity and amplify their devotion to the team, club, school, university, or business they are representing.

Team History

I have coached organizations where the players, some who had been on the team for an extended period of time, knew next to nothing about the organization or school they were representing. This is a tragedy. As coach, it is your responsibility to educate your team (both athletes and staff) so they have a basic knowledge of your organization's history. Establishing this allows your players to build that mindset that your team has a past and future. This creates a linear style of thinking which instills a message among the players that "there was a team before me, and the team will be here after me." In turn, this promotes the mentality that "the team is larger than me or any player." This kind of thinking encourages athletes to put the team ahead of the individual and diminishes the threat of selfishness.

The easiest method for sharing your team's history is to simply sit your players and staff down and educate them on the organization's past with a classroom session. Introduce them to the history of your program: when the organization was established, notable players and staff, and major victories and events, in addition to anything else you deem relevant. Give your team the opportunity to ask questions if they wish—some of them may surprise you.

If you are a new team, have a very short history, or are trying to relaunch your program completely—your organizational identity is you! New teams serve as the foundation for all future teams. Whether you win the championship or just win one game, how your team handles themselves will set the bar for years to come. Make sure that your players know, accept, and embrace the responsibility of being trailblazers.

Inspiration in the Locker Room

If you have a team locker room, do not hesitate to enhance it with photos and accolades from your team's history. Anything from championship photos to mementos of other defining moments can serve as a constant reminder of team identity and goals. Moreover, it can easily create a joint motivation for your players to become "part of the legacy" in the future. The pride you will see on your players' faces if they are fortunate enough to make the locker-room wall will last a lifetime.

Most locker rooms have a common area where players get dressed. That area is an opportunity for you to create lasting images through photographs of past teams and heroes, slogan banners with inspirational messages, or quotes that the players will see all year while preparing for the game.

Another spot to think about is wherever your players exit the room to the field, court, or rink. Flood the walls with photos of past championships or a chronological list of your team's accomplishments over the years. This will remind your players they are part of a legacy. Also, ask yourself and your other coaches the question, "What is the last thing we want to see before going out to play?" Take time in the off-season to create campaigns or maintain a game-by-game theme with a fitting quote or message to put above the door as you exit. Explain to your players that when they leave the room, this is the mentality that is expected of them.

In many of my locker rooms I have the slogan "Team, Teammates, Self" and "Accountability" right in the common area. I always want to make sure those ideals are never far from the player's sight and mind. While they are essential concepts to success, I am often surprised how often both players and coaches refer to those banners throughout the year.

Whether you have a large or small budget, coaches should take the initiative to have elements of identity like these created. Something as simple as a word poster with a logo or photos from the past for your locker room can be created easily via an online or local print store. If your team or school has a marketing, communications, or promotions department, don't hesitate to work with them to create something unique and special for your team. This is an important concept, to have these ideological reminders to help your teams rally around inspirational themes.

Inspiration out of the Locker Room

One of the things I do early on, when getting involved with an organization, is meet with their media/creative team. If a team does not have a media presence, I urge that one be created. I have found through my experience that having a strong relationship with a team's media group can help to enhance both your team's identity while also boosting the confidence of your players.

I try to create and incorporate a "media day" immediately after training camp ends. During this time, players all have their head shots taken along with short promo videos of them in their jerseys and equipment, both as individuals and as small groups. In addition, I also ask that every player does a five- to ten-minute interview on camera to discuss what it means to be part of the team and what fans can expect of them this year. I usually end the day with taking the team photo.

This collected content is usually shared by team media with the fan base early in the year (giving them a tangible con- nection to the players). I also have used it for motivational videos throughout the year. It's never a bad idea to remind the players of their determination and thoughts from early in the season as the grind and repetition of games and prac- tice can sometimes wear them out. Moreover, most players like to see themselves and teammates in the spotlight. It re- minds them that they matter to the team and organization.

The truth is, involving the media with your team helps to boost the confidence of players while also establishing their identity in photos and video. On top-level professional teams, this type of function is done automatically but on many semi-pro, collegiate, and high school teams it is not a common occurrence. Allowing your athletes to emulate the experience of a professional team will only amplify their belief in your group as a top-level organization. Take the time to do this and make your players feel special. It will pay off!

The Impact of Past Players

Throughout the season, invite players from the past to come to practice and/or games, and share stories from their time in the organization. The opportunity for your athletes to meet former players face to face can add a much deeper perspective to this type of identity. While images and information are great reminders, a living, breathing embodiment allows your players to create a more tangible connection to the organization's history. The ability for your players to think, "This person has been there and understands what we are going through," can be very powerful for morale.

GEOGRAPHIC IDENTITY

It's a given that your athletes know the name of the city or school they represent. The question that should be asked, from the professional level down to middle school, is: Do they know anything about that city or school, or the surrounding region? If you ask your players this question, their answers might surprise you. Allowing your players and staff to learn about the surrounding area or educational venue that you represent adds another layer to your team's overall identity.

Take a look at international competitions such as the Olympics or World Championships to understand how important this locational identity is. Athletes at world competitions are seldom paid outside of endorsements, yet they play with the same or in some cases with heightened passion, compared to their normal league performance. Why is this? It's because they have the opportunity to represent their country.

No matter what level you coach, from youth sports to professional, this type of identity exists. Middle and high school teams have it easiest, as it is likely your athletes are from the town where the school is located. However in college, while a number of your student athletes may be from surrounding towns, others come from around the country. In professional sports, it's rare that any of the players are from the city they represent. No matter which of these brackets you fit, take the time to educate your players about the location they now play for and invite them to embrace the community representation concept. It can be very powerful.

For example, if you operate in an area that has seen better days, encourage your players to realize that they have the opportunity and privilege to serve as a beacon of hope for that community through their effort, as much as for their ability to win. Perhaps you represent a city that is booming. Invite and challenge your team to be a part of that area's exposure and positive growth. Maybe your team is located in a small town or community. Challenge them to make a name for themselves and put the area on the map. No matter where you live, search for the aspects that make your community unique and ways players can make an impact beyond just their athletic prowess.

In addition to educating them, give your players the ability to connect with your location's story firsthand. Look for community outreach programs, such as reading to students or teaching your game at local schools. Outside of education, look for opportunities to get involved with other local and municipal programs such as fire and police departments. This will allow your team to interact with locals and understand at a deeper level what it means to represent the local community.

Fans

Interacting with fans can sometimes be a touchy subject for coaches, so I'll make it very clear. When it comes to how the game is played, you never have to listen to any fan's opinion. You and your staff were hired to make those decisions. However, organizations should strive to make sure that fans are heard and are part of the club at every other level. For this reason, the people who attend and pay (with money or their time) to see your team play should absolutely become part of your overall identity.

Athletes are extremely competitive and selfish by nature—they have to be. No matter if they are at the top of their game or just starting, at one point in their lives they were a young fan watching the game. Don't be afraid to connect with that idea on a small level and inspire them to remember why they started playing in the first place.

Moreover—no matter how much we embrace or deny it, we all love playing to a big crowd. It creates energy that can in turn give your team a boost. There is a reason why in most sports competitions the home record is always better than the away. Knowing and connecting to the people in the stands, even if just by signing autographs after the game or doing community outreach, goes a long way not just for your fans but also for your players. It helps your players have a deeper understanding of what or whom they are playing for besides the win.

TEAM IDENTITY

In each season, your team's ability to know and understand what they stand for as individuals and as a group is imperative for both maintaining the bond and winning. Often referred to as a team's "character," this form of identity solidifies the foundation for how your players will deal with adversity throughout the year.

Unlike the other levels of identity, this form cannot be taught or explained directly to the players. Some coaches make the mistake of having too much control over a team by telling them what they must accomplish. Let them tell you what they think they *can* accomplish and then continually motivate them to achieve and surpass those goals. Their buy-in will be much greater. In addition, never make the mistake of thinking that your athletes automatically have predetermined goals for what they want to accomplish during the year. Talk to them about their goals and help them set meaningful ones.

> **Your team's ability to know and understand what they stand for as individuals and as a group is imperative for both maintaining the bond and winning.**

Before your season even starts, take the initiative to help your players establish both individual and group goals by sitting with them one-on-one and as a team to ask questions about what they desire to accomplish this season. In addition, explore what motivates and demotivates your players. Managers and coaches often make the mistake of thinking everyone is motivated the same way they were/are. Different people are motivated in different ways. For example, some athletes are motivated by winning and others by money. At the same time, some are motivated by being yelled at, while others are discouraged by the same approach. As a coach, if you don't know what drives your players, how can you be an effective leader?

Before the start of the season, I have all my athletes fill out a questionnaire. This not only helps them to begin thinking about the goals they want to set for the season but also provides our coaching staff with a better understanding of the minds of our players. Throughout the season, we can refer to these surveys to track progress and reinvigorate an athlete when needed.

Here are some example questions I have used in the past:

- How many points do you see yourself scoring this season?
- What will (could) keep you from accomplishing your goals this season?
- What are your strengths as an athlete?
- What are your weaknesses as an athlete?
- How can you improve as an athlete?
- How will you contribute to the team outside of point production?
- What motivates you?
- What demotivates you?
- Why did you choose to play for this team?
- How can we help you achieve your goals this season?

In addition to individual goals, establishing team goals early will serve as a benchmark to your players' understanding of what they will be accountable for as a unit—for the entire season.

- Where do you think we can/want to finish this season?
- What are our strengths as a team?
- What are our weaknesses as a team?
- What can we do as a team to improve?
- How do we define success as a team?
- What can keep us from accomplishing our goals?

Allowing players to answer questions like these will give them ownership over their goals and help hold themselves accountable to their goals throughout the course of the season.

4
ACCOUNTABILITY

THE PERFECT TEAM

Imagine coaching a team where all of your players strive to be students of the game. A team where blame is not placed on one person but shared by everyone. A team where minds are more focused on finding solutions to problems rather than avoiding them. This type of team views accountability as a responsibility instead of an option. Creating this type of team atmosphere is more within your reach than you may think.

If the concept of communal trust is the beating heart of your team and identity is your team's character or personality, accountability is your team's brain. The word accountable is defined as the obligation to justify actions or decisions. When we apply this to sports, accountability is measured by your players' and staff's ability, and perhaps more importantly by their desire, to take responsibility for their actions and the actions of their teammates. When a strong commitment to accountability exists within the team, you will find that when problems arise, your athletes will try to solve the issues and improve instead of avoid them. This breeds an environment where the growth and improvement of individual players as athletes and intellectuals—in addition to the team's bond as a cohesive unit—accelerates.

A team without personal accountability will find excuses for mistakes and losses; team members with accountability will look for solutions.

Accountability in general is an aspect of each individual's personality, and not necessarily everyone is born with it. It needs to be learned and then emphasized. Coaches sometimes subscribe to the thought process that "players will think what they want to think and I have no control over that." This is not true. Accountability is a learned behavior and you have the ability as coach to help your players develop an accountable acumen throughout the season.

In any game or season, no one play or game is truly responsible for winning or losing. Sure, a last-second drive or incredible display of athleticism can give you the yards, runs, goals, and/or points you needed to come out on top, but those events are only one part of the contest's entire story. In truth, winning and losing are the results of the culminated efforts and plays of every member of your team and staff. When your team understands and adopts this concept, every person inside your locker room not only has a job, but also plays a vital role in the winning effort.

Make sure your team understands that each person has an important and unique role he or she must uphold to enable the group to win together. When the members of your team are accountable to those roles, they will strive to improve their overall performance. This can result in your star athletes playing at their absolute best, younger players making key plays when called upon, veteran players selflessly sharing their experience with the rest of the group, and assistant coaches providing valuable insight at key moments, among other desirable behaviors from the team.

When teaching the ideals of accountability to your team, there are several tools you can use to help players fully grasp this concept.

Internal Dialogue

Before we dive in, I want to be clear: when speaking about internal dialogue, I am not talking about a player's actual game day performance. An athlete's ability to play the game is the most vital role he or she has in helping the team win. While attitude and mental stability can affect physical play, sometimes athletes just have bad days at the office. If one of your players is having a poor showing or continues to make the same mistake over and over again, as a coach, you must do what you feel is right to deal with that situation.

We all have an internal dialogue. Sometimes it's the voice inside our head that tells us to "push harder" or adversely, to "give up." Other times it can make us question and be critical of the choices and actions of our friends and leaders. These private thoughts are the most unfiltered and honest views that anyone can have. For athletes, what this voice says to them throughout the course of a season can make or break their confidence and the way they perform. If your players aren't able to recognize when they are having negative thoughts and turn them into positive motivations, this lack of control can considerably affect their ability to compete in games throughout the season.

Let me give you an example. It's late in the game and a player on your team causes a turnover that ultimately ends up costing you the contest. What do your players think internally? The answer to this question can be drastically different, depending on the person. One player may think, "I should have done more to be in a better position for my teammate," while another may think, "Wow, I'm glad I didn't cause that turnover," while another thinks, "My teammate just cost us the game." Moreover, what are the players on your sideline thinking? It could range from "I'm glad I'm not out there" to "I should have been out there because that wouldn't have happened."

While these are starkly different responses to common situations, the truth is, none of these responses are abnormal in sports. As a coach, it is your job to challenge and inspire your players as individuals to have an internal dialogue that is conducive to helping your team win. The best way to teach them to do this borrows the same technique we use to teach our respective sports: practice.

This starts by making sure that you are vocally encouraging your team to give themselves the right messages during key points in the game. "*We* must do more to support each other in these situations" is much more powerful to your team than "*You* need to make that play." From the point of view of your players, messages such as these will put the accountability to play better on everyone and not just on one player. Understandably, there will be times when individuals must be singled out, but knowing when and how to do so is important. Immediately after a play has gone wrong and tensions are high may not be the best time.

It also helps to recognize situations that trigger your player's internal dialogue. More often than not, these moments happen during stoppages in play. It may be after a major event such as a score or a minor event such as a bad pass, a penalty, or an individual play. Depending on what sport you coach, breaks in play may be very brief or fairly long. No matter the length, always be willing to ask yourself what your team's mental state might be after a play. If you are feeling pressure in the bottom of your gut, odds are your players are too. At the same time, if you are feeling overly ecstatic about a good play, it's a good bet your players are also. The benefit of being in touch with these feelings is that it prevents your group from becoming too high or too low emotionally. Successful teams strive to be even-keeled, no matter the situation. Don't hesitate to remind your team of this during shifts in the game. Trust that you know the nuances of your game enough to recognize situations where mental momentum can shift easily.

One of the most difficult communication tactics for you as a coach and leader to achieve is making sure that the messages you give to your players span both a positive and negative temperament, not just one or the other. Constant negative reinforcement over time will only position your athletes with the goal of performing for you above the overall team. While having players who strive to please you is a plus, it is a lost concept if they aren't putting the team first. At the same time, constant positive reinforcement will reduce competitiveness and position your players with the goal of playing for themselves over the team as a whole. Make sure that it is clear before every game that performances will be gauged by the coaching staff on a team level before on an individual level.

In regards to teaching your players to create an accountable internal dialogue, it is very important to understand what motivates each player. Calling out a player who doesn't respond well to that type of motivation in front of the entire team can be detrimental to that player's state of mind and can also have residual effects on the rest of the group, especially if a team bond exists. If we are dealing with some-one's private thoughts, exposing them could be seen as an act of betrayal or a break of trust on your part as coach. When dealing with individual accountability, teaching should be done broadly to the entire team or behind closed doors, one-on-one.

The Culture of Accountability

When you think of accountability from a team perspective, it comes down to every player in the locker room shar-ing the mindset that "I play for the person sitting next to me." When this kind of thought process exists, it creates a culture of accountability for your team. When this doesn't exist, you will get players putting alternative incentives first, such as competing for playing time, gaining approval of the coaching staff, or even (in pro sports) benefitting their contract negotiations during the season, which takes every-one's focus away from the game. These are all distractions from winning. In order to win, the team must be focused on doing whatever they can to support each other while having the best performance possible as individual players. I'm not saying that these distractions won't still happen when an accountability culture does exist, but they won't be priori-tized ahead of the team.

In sports, ego is always a factor—whether it reveals itself as the swagger of your best player knowing how good he or she is or the inevitable feeling of power that comes with being a coach. When it comes to the competitive nature of athletes, strong personalities are inevitable in any locker room. If too many of your players have a narcissistic mindset, your room can quickly become a pressure cooker.

The ability for all team members, regardless of experience or skill level, to exhibit selfless behavior is a major contributor to your team's collective competitive advantage.

As the coach, you lead the way with this kind of unselfish thinking. You must instill in your team members the concept of playing for the person seated next to them before thinking about themselves. When an entire team buys into this concept, external accountability exists.

Ultimately, creating this ability starts when you begin choosing players for your team. If you are picking players who have a "me before we" attitude, you are creating an uphill battle for yourself. It's better to have a team of talented players with impeccable work ethics and who understand the concept of accountability than to have a group of exceptional players who don't. Look for the right type of person for your team, as much as you look for the right type of talent.

How do you pick those players out of the bunch? Simple: you ask questions. If a player says he is motivated by winning and teamwork versus getting paid and getting more playing time, that's a pretty good indicator of what type of person he is. Adversely, if a player says he or she is demotivated by a lack of teamwork or selfishness, it's another positive indication they are the type of person you are look-ing for. If you don't ask the questions, you will never know.

Self-Discipline

Once you have instilled in your players a strong understand-ing of accountability, maintaining that ideal throughout the season is a matter of self-discipline. Your players' ability to stay mentally sharp regardless of the situation is a trait that can mean the difference between being a champion or a runner-up.

One of the hardest things for any team to do in sports is to play the entire game with no mental breaks. I am not speak-ing about perfect play, which is impossible. I am talking about the ability for your team to display complete focus from the start of the game to the finish. If your coaching staff and team strive for this each game, it will lead to great success.

As a coach, I explain this ideal way of performing at the start of the season. Ice hockey games are three periods of twenty minutes—therefore, I expect my team to strive to play 60 full minutes each night, no matter the score or situ-ation. To reinforce this idea, we have a sign above the exit door of the locker room that has our team crest followed by "60 MINUTES!" This serves as a constant reminder to the group of what we are striving for: perfect mental discipline for the entire game, no matter what adversity we face.

Developing this ability often starts with the small things, like showing up to team meetings and functions early or on time, eating right, and taking care of your body. It also means making sure that players face the coach when he or she is addressing the group. It builds to bigger standards, such as studying and absorbing tactics and information from a playbook and executing drills at practice with the same intensity as one would during a game. These are all examples of team focus and self-discipline. Players should strive to be flawless in these small disciplines throughout the season, without excuses.

Making sure that your team learns and displays these mannerisms during the season is critical preparation for big games and postseason competition. Championship-level games bring out a heightened level of play and awareness for most teams. They also can bring an amplified level of emotion and atmosphere. When so much is on the line, these added aspects can knock a team off course or empower them to greatness. In playoff situations, even the smallest advantage can mean the difference between winning and losing.

Teams that practice strong mental discipline and focus throughout the season will be better prepared for big game situations than teams without that experience.

BUILDING ACCOUNTABILITY

The very first on-ice practice I ran as a head coach was done with no pucks.

I believe that in the game of hockey, giving a full 60-minute effort is the hardest thing to do. With all the distractions, emotions, and general highs and lows of a game, having a full squad of players who can maintain their full mental and physical focus for the entire game is nearly impossible. With this belief, I asked this question: If our players did not know what it meant to work hard for 60 minutes in practice, how would they ever know how to do so in games?

Sixty minutes of hard skating is not akin to a morning jog. It is literally the equivalent of asking someone to sprint as hard as they can for 45–60 seconds over and over again, with very little rest between. It is, in a word, "hell."

Prior to the practice, I had a meeting with the team and explained what, and more importantly, *why* they were being asked to do this. I explained my philosophy behind the 60 minutes concept and how understanding what it would take to complete this practice would make them accountable to their play all season.

While the practice was extremely taxing on the players physically (more than one player lost their lunch), the results were incredible. We overachieved the entire season. However, the game results were not the most astonishing thing. Several times throughout the season, after losses or close games, I heard players in the locker room say, "We didn't work for the full 60 tonight, boys, and we know that we can." Perhaps even more surprising was that multiple times throughout the season, my captains approached me and asked to have the team skate for 60 minutes *again* at practice, in order to remind them of what they had gone through at the start of the season.

Their understanding that the team had more to give and that they were willing to do whatever it would take to win was full accountability. The 60-minute skate had evolved from a fitness test into a team-rallying call toward victory.

5
LEADERSHIP

When I was a freshman in college, the captain of my hockey team was asked before a big game what his leadership would mean to the team on that night. I'll never forget his response. He said, "I am just one guy. Tonight I am expecting everyone to be a leader on the ice." That short statement had an immediate and also a lifelong impact on me. While we all looked up to this leader, both figuratively and literally (he was 6'7" on skates), until that moment I didn't realize leadership is a shared responsibility—no matter who has the title on their jersey.

As a coach, do you understand what makes a good leader within your team? Do you base it on skill, character, seniority, or other factors? Should this leader be vocal or lead by example? Does this person need to be selected by you or elected by your team? No matter what your approach is to the process of placing one or several of your athletes into leadership positions, the truth is, what makes great team captains are great coaches and what makes great coaches are great captains. Both must rely on each other throughout the season and, most importantly, share a trust and understanding that cannot be broken. This connection is critical to maintaining and strengthening the team bond.

CHOOSING YOUR CAPTAINS

Perhaps your team already has a great—or in some cases legendary—captain in place. Now is the time to start grooming others to step into that role if needed—because inevitably, some factor (graduation, retirement, injury, trades, etc.) will transfer that captain from that position temporarily or for good. The best preparation for a leadership role is to work with and learn from the current leader. Just like the coaching staff, a captain and his or her alternates are another team within the team.

How you choose leaders for your team can vary depending on the sport you play, where you are in the course of the year, and the current status of your team.

The person chosen as the leader of your team must understand that they have the responsibility of representing the players, the coaching staff, and the organization as a whole.

They must also understand that they have an obligation to mentor players that may be future leaders. That is not a calling to take lightly. It is up to you as the coach to decide how and when to award a leadership role.

Many factors can make a great leader for your team. Instead of trying to explain the "right" parameters for choosing a captain, I think it's more important to identify those characteristics that cannot be the only or the primary decision-making factors.

Athletic Skill

It's a common misconception that the best player on your team will automatically be the best leader. Athletic skill is a barometer of talent, not leadership. While exceptional play is exciting and inspiring for any team, it does not encompass the full spectrum of great leadership. Leadership is as much a learned skill as the talent needed to play your sport—and the most important leadership behaviors must be present off the field, court, or rink as well as on it. Entrusting a skillful player with leadership before they are ready can cause a decline in their talent level, and possibly negative feelings toward the team. Think about it—you would never expect an inexperienced player to regularly perform at the level of a superstar. Expecting an inexperienced leader to lead effectively is just as unlikely. If you are considering a top talent on your team for the leadership role, make sure they feel empowered to play their best on the field before you ask them to be a leader off the field.

Popularity

I am not a big fan of letting the players decide who their captain will be. As coach, you have the right to choose the person you want to work with in that role. There are many ways to empower your players to feel that they have a voice in the room, and choosing the captain is not one I recommend. You may feel differently—however, as a championship coach, I feel strongly about choosing team leadership. As a business leader, you may consider this as well.

You must always protect the idea that you are the chief person in charge of the team. Allowing your players to elect someone into a leadership position will inevitably challenge that authority at some point. With that said, there is nothing wrong with speaking to your players, one on one, about who they believe would make a good leader. Their opinion very much matters in helping you decide, but it should not be the only factor.

While there may be players in your locker room that everyone loves, it does not mean they are fit to be leaders of the entire team. Athletic leaders on your team, like coaches, must have the respect of the other players over their admiration. Captains have to make very hard and sometimes unpopular choices during the season that affect their teammates. Entrusting a popular player with this can easily work against the team if they are not ready or willing to make the tough decisions.

While well-liked players can play key roles in keeping your locker room in good spirits, they can also use their influence in a negative way if they feel the group is being treated unfairly. Captains must always respect the balance of their role between the coaching staff and the players. If that scale tips too far toward the coaching staff, your players will stop listening to their leader. If it goes the other direction, you may be looking at a mutiny.

Seniority

Do you have a player that has been with the organization longer than anyone else? This does not automatically qualify them to be your team leader. While older players bring a lot of experience and knowledge to your team, they can sometimes be outspoken and have a false sense of where they fit into the chemistry and hierarchy of the team. Entrusting a senior player with leadership before they are ready can lead to public disagreements that will force your players to choose between the captain and the coach.

The mindset of a player approaching the end of his or her high school, collegiate, or professional career can vary drastically, depending on the person. Some have a hard time accepting that their time with the team and possibly the game is coming to an end, and they may strive to play a role that was better suited to them earlier in their career. It is very important that players in this position, especially professional athletes, understand that you want them to play to their current strengths to best help the team instead of trying to emulate the player they were years ago.

At the same time, some veteran players accept that their time in the game is limited and want to make a positive impact in any way possible for as long as they are able. No matter the situation, it's OK for game styles to change and evolve over time in sport, and age is the ultimate factor in determining that. Make sure your veteran players understand it is imperative for them to be who they are now, before you entertain the idea of putting them in a leadership position.

Necessity

If you are required by your organization or league to designate a team leader but there isn't a comfortable choice—pick several rather than just one. Just like player development, thrusting players into the leadership limelight can have dramatic consequences on their psyche and sometimes even their overall career if they are not ready. I find the best thing to do when no player emerges as a leader is to share the captaincy role within the entire team. Each game, select a different player to list as "captain." Over time, one of your players may take to the role and if not, the team will continue to rely on each other to bear the responsibility.

If you think someone you are considering to be a leader fits into one of these above categories but you aren't sure if they are ready for the responsibility, consider awarding them the alternate captain spot and have them serve under the existing captain. None of these types of players are bad for your team, they just may need a bit more guidance in order to mature into the type of leader you want.

The player that usually is most deserving of the "C" is usually the one who needs it the least. Captaincy is an honor that is earned through collective experience and is not something that should be sought after as a trophy. An overall mix of all the ideals mentioned above: talent, popularity, necessity, seniority, and other traits help to form a great leader. When you mix these ideals with trust, resolve, accountability, selflessness, and determination, you get character—the consummate qualification for any true leader.

COACH'S ROLE TO THE CAPTAIN

When it comes to leadership relationships in your locker room, none is more important than that between you (and the coaching staff) and the captain(s) of the team. In order to find success as a team, coaches and captains must empower and enable each other continually throughout the year.

A captain or leader without the strong support of his or her coach and the coaching staff is just a player with a meaningless letter stitched on their jersey.

Make sure your coaching staff clearly understands where they fit in the hierarchy in relation to the team captain. Also make it clear to all that you value and rely on your captain. It is your responsibility to enable your captain to lead your team on the field of battle. Just as in war, soldiers cannot be expected to fight and win if they do not believe those leading them have the trust of those at the top.

You should have weekly meetings with your captain(s) and staff to assess both the team's performance and mindset, and discuss any issues that may be facing the team. In addition, you should keep your captain(s) abreast of any information that will impact your team that you feel comfortable sharing. Doing so will give you a chance to get his or her thoughts on how it will affect the player population, in addition to giving your captain time to mentally prepare for any changes. For example, if there is going to be player movement due to injury, trades, or signings, letting your captain know will help you prepare the team for the changes. While you do not need to tell your captain everything, keeping them in the loop will make them feel like a larger and more important part of the team and in turn make them a better leader. No one likes to be blindsided if it can be avoided.

No matter what level your team plays at, your ability to be a mentor, regardless of age gap or experience gap, is what will help to fortify the relationship between you and your captain. For middle and high school coaches, this may mean taking more time to explain the importance of education in addition to athletics, while in college and pro it may take the form of emphasizing the aspects of professionalism at work. No matter what the situation, make sure to adapt your mentorship style to help your leader be in the best overall position as a person and player to be an effective leader.

This is a poem that I give to every captain who serves under my tenure as a coach. It has inspired me throughout my life as a player, coach, son, and father. I believe it speaks to the internal dialogue that players should have while also encompassing what it takes to be a good leader, teammate, and person.

"IF" BY RUDYARD KIPLING

If you can keep your head when all about you
Are losing theirs and blaming it on you,
If you can trust yourself when all men doubt you,
But make allowance for their doubting too;
If you can wait and not be tired by waiting,
Or being lied about, don't deal in lies,
Or being hated, don't give way to hating,
And yet don't look too good, nor talk too wise:

If you can dream—and not make dreams your master;
If you can think—and not make thoughts your aim;
If you can meet with Triumph and Disaster
And treat those two impostors just the same;
If you can bear to hear the truth you've spoken
Twisted by knaves to make a trap for fools,

Or watch the things you gave your life to, broken,
And stoop and build 'em up with worn-out tools:

If you can make one heap of all your winnings
And risk it on one turn of pitch-and-toss,
And lose, and start again at your beginnings
And never breathe a word about your loss;
If you can force your heart and nerve and sinew
To serve your turn long after they are gone,
And so hold on when there is nothing in you
Except the Will which says to them: 'Hold on!'

If you can talk with crowds and keep your virtue,
Or walk with Kings—nor lose the common touch,
If neither foes nor loving friends can hurt you,
If all men count with you, but none too much;
If you can fill the unforgiving minute
With sixty seconds' worth of distance run,
Yours is the Earth and everything that's in it,
And—which is more—you'll be a Man, my son!

CAPTAIN'S ROLE TO THE COACH

While as coach you have been entrusted with running the entire team, you will not get far if the players in your locker room don't believe in you. Your athletic leaders are the conduits to making sure this belief endures throughout the season. Always strive to keep your team leaders in the loop with your thoughts and goals for the season as early as possible. Make sure to also ask for their point of view and thoughts during your team meetings. This shows them and the team that you are listening and value their input. A captain who feels he or she has a voice is more likely to speak than one who does not feel their opinions are heard or valued.

A captain should not be expected to have blind allegiance to the coach. Instead, they should be asked to have a mutual respect and understanding for your respective roles and how they apply to the team. Captains should recognize that they don't always have to agree with your thoughts on running the team, but they must respect that you are the authority. This aspect of the coach-captain relationship can be vital when teams go through a rough patch.

When players get disgruntled or begin to challenge tactics, your captain may be the key to adjusting their attitudes in the right direction to benefit the team. Unless you are incredibly fortunate, at some point in the season your team will hit a rut. It may come in the form of a losing streak or losing a big game. During these times it is not uncommon for players and coaches to ask questions more than look for answers. More than any other time, at these times your leaders must stand and support you as the coach. A good ship captain cannot abandon his crew during a crisis any more than the crew can abandon the captain—especially if he or she is the only one who knows how to steer the ship.

Once again, the level you coach at will mean different things to the captain's ability to work with you. We cannot expect a teenager to have the same emotional poise and stature as an adult, and at the same time, we cannot expect a grown-up to have the same innocence as a child. Make sure you take into account the experience level of your captain when setting your expectations of their responsibilities to you.

HELPING PLAYERS UNDERSTAND THEIR PLACE ON THE TEAM

A player's understanding of their position on the team is as important to the outcome as a soldier's job in battle—everyone must know who they report to and who to obey without question. If one person goes rogue or does not perform their duty, others may perish. Your players should take the view that earning a position on the team is a responsibility and a badge of honor they should strive to achieve.

Never underestimate the power of sitting down with any player and making sure they understand what their role is on the team. Giving them this renewed purpose will result in a better relationship and improved performance. Adversely, if you do not take the time to help establish a person's role, you cannot expect an athlete without a purpose to stay motivated for long.

There are several types of players on any team: superstars (highly skilled athletes), rookies (developing players), role players (those who show up and do their job day in and day out), veterans (older players who have been in the game for a while), and others. Some players engage with their roles quickly, while others develop over time. Helping your athletes recognize and embrace their role on the team is an important part of establishing layers of leadership within your locker room.

While some players will understand and embrace their role from the start of the season, others may not or, worse, may see themselves in a role that doesn't fit with your plans. If you are dealing with a player who does not understand or agree with the role they have been given, sit down with them and discuss their position. Ask why they feel they are better suited for another role and make sure to listen—they may present a surprisingly convincing case. At the same time, make sure that you explain why you feel that player is suited for the role you have designed for them.

How your athletes are utilized is ultimately up to you.

A player does not need to like the role in order to understand it and perform.

Making sure your players understand where you are coming from and vice versa will only empower both of you in your respective roles.

A player's age and/or maturity level can also heavily influence their ability to buy into the concept of having a role within the team. When coaching student-athletes, discussions about player roles are the perfect place to inject the thought that "the team is not a democracy." While this idea may not always be popular with players, it must be established in order to help a player fully understand that you will have the final say on how they fit into the team. While their lack of any say on the matter may be hard to swallow (and equally hard to enforce), know that you are doing your players a service as the lesson often transcends athletics and in turn prepares your student-athletes for entering the challenges of the "real world."

For professional athletes, the concept of having a role is the same as having a job title.

Players have to be accountable to the job they are given even if it may not be the job they want. Make sure to encourage and motivate your athletes to excel in their role while also leaving the door open for them to expand, exchange, or evolve into another role in the future.

Developing Players

Younger players always vary in skill level. Some may be ready for big playing minutes right away, while others may need multiple seasons before they get comfortable. In either case, fledgling, energetic athletes are often eager to play as much as possible. Most are coming from a situation where they were one of the best players on their previous team and received more playing time due to their age or skill level. Knowing how to challenge their hunger correctly can be extremely beneficial to the team.

Go out of your way to meet with these players before the season and give them realistic expectations for the year. This encompasses both short- and long-term goals. Also allow them to ask questions. Meetings like these will allow you to learn what areas of a rookie's game (tactics, skill, nutrition, fitness, etc.) need improvement, in addition to concerns they may have about joining the team.

It is not uncommon for young players to receive limited playing time during their first season to build experience and get a feel for the game at a higher level. Both you and the veteran players on your team should explain that being an inexperienced young player is completely normal, and they should embrace the position. Moreover, explain that rushing into the spotlight is a mistake that has claimed the careers of many undeveloped athletes.

If you want your team to have a winning tradition over time, don't feel the need to hurry any player to the spotlight unless you are certain they are ready. No matter what their skill level, there will be a mental, physical, or tactical learning curve for new players. Make sure your young players understand this and help them create a plan to grow in their position.

Role Players

While teams have captains, in truth, leadership can come from many different players on the team. When building a group based on trust and accountability, all players truly share the leadership role in some form or another. If you coach a middle school or high school team, your second string role players serve a valuable purpose in providing backup, and you must communicate to them the importance of their role to the team. If you coach a professional team, let's briefly put aside the notion that the bottom half of your lineup is "replaceable," whether it be by trades or new signings. You may find that some players are more irreplaceable than you think.

As coaches, we rely heavily on the effort of our skilled players to inspire the rest of the team to put points on the scoreboard. We hear over and over again that "our best players need to be our best players in order to win"—and it's true.

While your skilled players may hold the key to success on the scoreboard, there is another type of competitor in the locker room that could potentially hold the same amount of significance to your team's success in the standings. Every team has one athlete (or more than one) who has a tremendous amount of determination, willpower, and motivation but just doesn't have the same amount of skill or talent as your top performers. This person is known as the "role player," and they are one of the most vital parts of a winning team.

Whether it be a grizzly old veteran who just doesn't have the same athleticism as in previous years or a hungry young player whose body and skill sets haven't fully matured yet, enabling this person to understand their position as a role player on the team is imperative. In essence, this player's work ethic, both on and off the field of play, will be what other players reference when determining how hard they need to work—a barometer for your team. It takes a special type of athlete to accept this responsibility. Your ability to utilize this silent leader to set the work ethic bar for your team is a major factor in finding long-term success.

Why is setting this bar important? There are many reasons. There are literally thousands of quotes about how important hard work is to creating winners. One of the most popular is a favorite of mine when dealing with this situation: "Hard work beats talent when talent doesn't work hard." The more effort your players put in athletically and mentally, the better the team will become throughout the season. Empowering your hardest worker to understand that their effort level sets the bar for the rest of your team is a very powerful tool.

> **Hard work beats talent when talent doesn't work hard.**

I'm sure that you have already started to formulate who this player is on your squad. They show up on time to every practice and game with a never-say-die attitude and do what they are told, in spite of barely being able to crack the lineup. You rarely if ever consider them as an option when the game is on the line, and you rarely notice their play unless they have done something wrong. At the same time, you know this person pours every ounce of energy they have into every drill and every play throughout the season. You know they will never miss a team function and will represent the organization the way you'd expect in a public setting.

Go out of your way to take the time to meet with this player on your team and explain that you are entrusting them with one of the most difficult but important roles on the team. Explain that they will be asked to continually work harder than everyone else with the understanding that they will probably get less playing time than the rest of the team and most likely never be put into the public spotlight. What the player can expect in return is the appreciation of the coaching staff and the full respect of his or her teammates for taking on this silent but major role in the team's success.

There are many ways to utilize players like this throughout the season to benefit the team. If you feel that one of the superstar players on your team is not working hard enough, your role player is the perfect catalyst to wake them up. For example, one tactic is to remove the top player from his position and replace him or her with your role player. Moves such as these send the message to your team that you value hard work over talent, especially when talent doesn't work hard. Another tactic is to place the player not working hard enough next to your role player on an endurance drill or exercise where willpower is required to succeed. Who comes in first on the drill is irrelevant. Your role player will undoubtedly push your skilled player(s), among others, to do more.

Just to be clear, I'm not asking you to play parent and shout, "Why can't you be more like this role player who works so hard?" That's not a tactic I would say never to use, but it puts a negative connotation on the situation and individualizes players over the team. Work with your coaching staff to search out the best ways to use the role player to have a positive impact on your team.

Veteran Players and Mentors

Everyone remembers and refers to their mentors throughout life. It is no different in regards to mentors in sports.

Players come and go for many reasons. Some retire; others graduate. Some advance to the next level; others get traded. Make sure that you explain to your seasoned athletes the responsibilities and importance of passing on a legacy.

Sustainability in regards to winning in sports over time is almost as elusive as a championship, unless you plan for it. Inspire your veteran players and team leaders to take younger players under their wing throughout the course of the year. This mentoring relationship will accelerate the development process for your younger players while also energizing your veteran players. Over time, you will find that establishing strong mentorship bonds within your program will benefit the overall organization, not to mention the careers of your athletes.

Having the senior players take out the newer players for a night on the town is not mentorship, that's just camaraderie. Mentorship in sports encompasses the passing of one's collective knowledge from an experienced player to a younger protégé. Attaching a strong role model to a younger athlete who shares the same position or style can dramatically accelerate their development while also validating the knowledge and leadership of an older player.

The Superstar

It's easy to pick out the most skilled players on any team after watching a few practices or games. Knowing what kind of person accompanies that skill cannot be seen with the naked eye. It is a common misconception that superstars have an easier time with their role than other members of the team. This is far from the truth. The most skilled players on your team in many ways have more pressure placed on their shoulders than anyone, even the coach. While they may have been endowed with a gift from the gods in regards to skill and ability, that does not automatically mean they will be able to perform in all situations.

Some superstars thrive in the limelight, while others are not built to handle that kind of attention. Some players are able to raise their game late in a contest when the score is tied or your team is trailing, while others make their mark during less stressful periods of the game. While top players will always garner more attention from the press, fans, and the team to some extent, knowing how to best position them in the superstar role comfortably is monumental to consistently getting their best performance.

Some teams have multiple superstars, while others have just one. When you have multiple players with remarkable ability on your squad, take the opportunity to position those who seem fearless in the spotlight and the timid in more of a supporting role. If you have just one player with talent above the rest, make sure that player understands, regardless of his or her temperament, that their success is dependent on the team's performance as a whole.

I have seen many situations where athletes who are not yet ready for the superstar's responsibility are pushed into the spotlight. Some are able to adapt and compete, but more often than not, the result is underperformance and an overall disappointing season. While top athletes will get the majority of play-

> **Make sure your top athletes are emotionally secure in their role, so they can exhibit their best play.**

ing time no matter how you position them, making sure they are emotionally secure in their role will create an environment for them to exhibit their best play.

Above all, when discussing with a player the responsibilities that come with the role of superstar, in addition to telling them you expect their best, establish an understanding that their performance on and off the field can directly affect how the rest of the team contributes to winning. In team sports, no one player can single-handedly win a game without the support of their teammates. One player can significantly contribute to the scoring or make a big play in a moment that matters, but no matter how much credit they receive for such actions, winning without his or her teammates is impossible.

To help your superstars understand this concept, explain to them the other team roles that exist, and how the performance of those roles will influence them. This will allow them to see both their importance as an athlete and how they fit into the overall team ecosystem—and enable them to win on a consistent basis.

For example, younger players tend to idolize superstars over veteran players. As veterans are often charged with mentoring developing players, a superstar can easily empower that calling by letting the younger player know the importance of the senior player's advice. Superstars can easily empower a role player who does not receive much playing time by acknowledging how their work ethic inspires them and the team. Perhaps most important is the ability for top players to bring out the best in other top players through healthy competition and the commitment to mutual goals. Truly great players understand that their talent is just one part of what it means to be a superstar.

ONE OF SPORTS' GREATEST CAPTAINS

When it comes to legendary hockey players, the first name most people think of is Wayne Gretzky. However, it might surprise people outside the sport that the first name most hockey fans think of when discussing legendary leaders is Mark Messier, the NHL's third all-time points leader behind Gretzky and Jaromir Jagr.

Both Gretzky and Messier played together for the Edmonton Oilers during their four-cup dynasty (over five years) in the 1980s, with Gretzky serving as the team captain. Gretzky was famously traded to the LA Kings during the 1988 off-season, and the following year Messier was tapped to succeed him as the team's captain. In 1990, in his first full year with the "C," Messier led the Oilers to their fifth Stanley Cup.

However, Messier's leadership, following the departure of the "great one," wasn't what made him the most famous team captain in NHL history. That title is attributed to the events of the 1994 Stanley Cup Playoffs.

In the Eastern Conference final that season, the New York Rangers (who traded for Messier in 1991) were playing their cross-river rivals, the New Jersey Devils. Down three to two in the series, Messier made a public proclamation, predicting his team would be victorious and force a game seven by saying, "We'll win tonight." The quote, which would go down in hockey history as "the guarantee," was famously posted on the back page of the *New York Post* for the entire world to see. Messier would later admit that he had said the quote in hopes his teammates would read it, not all of Manhattan.

What happened that night was something out of a storybook. With the pressure of an entire city on his back, Messier scored three goals for the hat trick, including an empty-net goal with seconds left. After scoring that final goal to seal the victory, Messier skated with open arms to his team's bench to embrace in victory with his teammates. The team would go on to win game seven and eventually the Stanley Cup in a seven-game test of wills against the Vancouver Canucks. New York had won its first Stanley Cup since 1940, and Messier would forever be remembered as the "Messiah" to New York hockey fans.

Messier's leadership was one of the most complete packages of any captain the sports world has seen. Prior to even being named a captain in the NHL, he had demonstrated the ability to inspire and motivate his teammates to greatness on multiple occasions. As his career progressed, he used his veteran experience as a teaching tool to young players and backed up what he preached with action. Above all, his passion for the game and winning was infectious to those around him.

Today the NHL annually presents the Mark Messier Leadership Award to a player who is a superior leader within the sport of hockey while also being a contributing member of society.

6

ADVERSITY

Almost every situation you face during a season whether good, bad, or indifferent is an opportunity to learn. While some are more apparent than others, the ability to recognize lessons that can be learned from every situation and pass on that information to your team is a skill every coach should constantly be developing. Your win/loss record is routinely the measuring stick to tell if you are good or bad at your job. In pure black and white terms this may be true, but in reality, how teams respond to victory and defeat is a much more important barometer of your ability as a coach and the overall strength of your team's bond.

Over the course of a season, nothing will tell you more about yourself or your team than how you or they deal with adversity.

In my experience, nothing builds character faster than the day-in, day-out grind of a season. Sports teams probably face more adversity in a week than most people see in a month. Some groups use these hardships as a rallying cry to strive forward together. Those that don't will crumble under the pressure.

Your team's ability to prepare for and conquer adversity is one of the most important skills to have in your arsenal. Teams that are ready for the emotional and physical roller-coaster ride that is a sports season will almost always have an edge on their opponent.

SET A NEW STANDARD: EMOTIONAL ENDURANCE

Some people see emotion as a weakness; I see it as more of a reality. Your team's ability to be in control of their emotions throughout the season is a massive factor to success. In life, highs and lows tend to come over the course of weeks, months, and years. In games, they come multiple times over the course of a few hours. Only in sports can we go from the thrill of scoring points, goals, runs, and wins to the despair of being scored on, injury, and defeat in the same day. Teaching your team how to stay emotionally even-keeled in every situation is an ongoing and tedious, yet essential, process.

In every game, there are moments you can use to better prepare your team to face adversity. For example, in most games, you will score points and get scored on. Simple concept, right? Every team I have been on has had a different response to this presumed circumstance of competition. Some would get overly thrilled every time we scored, and others barely showed any excitement at all. And also when getting scored against—some teams would fall into a pit of despair while others would shrug it off with no problem. On other teams, the players' reactions to these events was split. Every group of people comes from multiple backgrounds and experiences, and players will respond to situations with different emotions.

As the players on your team change every year, so will the way the collective group responds to adversity. It is up to you to continually adapt the way you coach to best correspond to this, not the other way around.

Your ability to teach your team to stay even-keeled, regardless of the score or situation, is as valuable as keeping your players healthy. Teams that don't adopt this concept tend to play hot and cold or, worse, fall apart completely. Any time you see a come-from-behind rally from the opposition or watch a team crumble late in the season and miss the playoffs, it is usually the result of the coaches' poor mental preparation.

When I coach, after any points are scored for or against, I ask my entire team, "What's the score?" The players know to always answer "zero-zero!" This is a constant reminder to the team that they are to stay focused on the task of winning and not to change their level of effort or focus based on the scoreboard.

Players naturally feed off of each other's emotions. For that reason, it is important that you create an environment where words like "resolve" and "purpose" are clearly understood.

Make sure your team knows that their ability to deal with adversity, both as individuals and as a group, is the characteristic that may determine whether they are a champion or the runner-up.

LOSING AS A TOOL FOR WINNING

On May 17, 1983, a young Wayne Gretzky sat in the "away" team locker room at Nassau Coliseum on Long Island, devastated. Minutes before, his Edmonton Oilers had lost the Stanley Cup Final to the New York Islanders in a four-game sweep.

One of the unfortunate things about losing at Nassau is that the away team must walk past the home team's locker room after the game. Embarrassed and heartbroken with the loss, the last thing Gretzky wanted in that moment was to pass by the Islanders locker room and see them celebrating their victory with the Stanley Cup. Nonetheless, Wayne composed himself, quickly showered, got dressed, and walked out of the locker room and through the corridor where the Islanders room waited. As he approached the room he told himself not to look in—just keep walking. But he couldn't help himself. He took a peek. He saw something that forever changed his mindset on what it takes to win.

Sitting in the center of the locker room, all alone, was the Stanley Cup. The Islander players, many who would become hall-of-famers in the coming years, were all slumped in their stalls laughing and smiling at the joy of winning their fourth Stanley Cup victory in a row. In spite of their victory, instead of dancing around the room with the Stanley Cup, each player was nursing their muscles with ice packs and medical wraps. The players clearly had given so much in order to win, there was literally not enough left to party.

As Gretzky continued to walk past the room, a curious thought entered his mind. "Those guys can't move, and I feel like I could play a few more games." Gretzky did not know it yet, but he was just one year away from his first of four Stanley Cups in five years and an amazing career that would dub him the undisputed greatest hockey player in history. However, this was the moment he would credit for years to come as when he learned what it takes to become a champion.

I am a firm believer that losing is the best teacher for teaching teams how to win. With that said, as a coach, I always want my players and staff to *hate* losing more than they like to win. I picked the word hate on purpose. I don't dislike losing, I don't dread it—I hate it. I hate it so much that every action I take as a coach is with the sole purpose of avoiding it.

Losing, more so than the opposing team, is your team's ultimate enemy. In *The Art of War*, Sun Tzu makes this statement:

> If you know your enemy and know yourself, you need not fear the result of a hundred battles. If you know yourself but not the enemy, for every victory gained you will also suffer a defeat. If you know neither the enemy nor yourself, you will succumb in every battle.

In short, only when you know your enemy will you understand how they can be defeated. I find players who share this mindset aren't just fierce competitors but also students of the game. When choosing players for your team, keep this in mind. While I wish all players were equipped with this mindset, some need a bit of instruction to get there.

One of my other favorite quotes when talking about defeat is, "I never lose. I win or I learn." This is an attitude that you and your team should aspire to throughout the season. Inspire your players to establish the attitude that failure, both as individuals and as a team, is an opportunity to learn. When you promote this way of thinking with a group that is accountable, progress is possible. A discouraged team that takes little or no time to learn is doomed to repeat the same mistakes over and over again.

In order to help achieve this way of thinking, have classroom sessions over the course of the season with your team to go over tactical errors and triumphs from the previous games. It is easy for coaches to make the mistake of assuming that something completely obvious to you during a game is automatically apparent. This is why classroom sessions are so important. There have been times in my career that I have been shocked when I had to explain a basic concept to a seasoned player. However, my approach is never sarcastic or condescending. In reality, I am happy to provide an athlete with a new tool and excited to see them apply it. Never assume your players know something that you think is "obvious." It may surprise you that what is "fundamental" to you is foreign to your players. Challenge your players to receive and interpret the information, not just watch the film to relive the moment.

The group's collective ability to recognize mistakes and losses as opportunities to learn is a huge asset and a key to being successful in all sports.

Creating a learning environment for your team will allow for continual improvement throughout the season so that you are playing at your best when a championship is on the line.

SLUMPS: DON'T PUT UNNEEDED PRESSURE ON YOURSELF OR THE TEAM

One of the worst types of adversity your team can face during a season is the inevitable slump. I refer to this period as "the lull." It can happen at any point of the season and in some cases more than once. No matter how good your team is playing in any given season, odds are at some point you will hit a losing streak. It is at these times that your team bond will be tested more than any other. Slumps are an inevitable but not unpredictable part of most sports seasons. The trick to navigating through the muddy waters of a slump is to be prepared to deal with them. If your work to develop a strong team bond has been successful, you are more than halfway there.

Although lulls can happen at any time during the season, I've noticed common patterns for three different types of slumps.

The Slow Start

For whatever reason, sometimes teams just can't get it going out of the starting gate. This may be due to a difficult schedule, athletes being in poor shape at the start of the season, or other reasons. Regardless, it is important that your team does not quit or give up too quickly on what you are trying to accomplish. Teams that have a slow start often end up chasing other teams for a good spot in the standings for the rest of the season.

The opportunity a slow start represents is that your team will develop a communal sense of resolve and understanding of how to play in high-pressure situations. Later in the season, this can be crucial to defeating teams that may have had an easier run in the league and therefore lack urgency. While an early-season slump can seem like a lifetime ago when pumping up for a playoff run, don't hesitate to remind your team of the adversity they overcame together at the start of the year.

The Mid-Season Lull

If you had to pick one of these three to go through, it would be this one, every time. A sports season is a long and arduous undertaking. At the end of the day, athletes are just people. They can get tired, bored, and overwhelmed. Season starts and finishes are exciting times for most teams. What about the middle? A few months of practices and games can take a toll on the body. Add in illness, injury, and possibly being away from family and friends, and anyone can feel worn out, no matter how good they are. Mid-season is prime time for most players to hit this wall (especially if you play a winter sport and the holidays happen to "get in the way").

Teams that are going through a mid-season lull should be reminded of the goals they set in the beginning of the season.

The opportunity represented by experiencing and escaping this kind of slump is that it will allow your team to reset mentally and give your players a fresh start to the second half of the season and into the playoffs.

The End-of-Season Slump

This is by far the worst of the three. No team wants to head into the postseason playoffs low on confidence. End-of-season slumps tend to happen to teams that have found success for a majority of the season but may have lost a few big games in the final quarter of the season. At first, players tend to shake these off, but if losses keep coming, despair can set in pretty fast.

Teams that are going through the end-of-season slump need to be reminded of the type of game they were playing up until the dark times started. Refer back to big games from earlier in the season, specifically when your team showed character and resolve, and ask your players to relive the emotions of those moments. Try not to push your team's championship goals too much during this time as it can add unneeded pressure to an already stressful situation. The opportunity represented by this slump is that your team will go into the post season understanding that they are not invincible and must commit to each other in order to win.

HOW TO PREPARE AND BREAK OUT OF A SLUMP

The key to preparing for a slump is knowing that one will inevitably happen and then recognizing the signs that one is on the horizon.

Losses happen, but as a coach you should be in touch with how a loss affects your team emotionally.

If you look around the room after a defeat and your players are just disappointed, there is no need to panic. If you look around the room and no longer see the fire in your players' eyes, it should set off a warning in your head.

Prepare from Day One

The process for this preparation starts on day one when you set the tone with your team. Make sure to explain that your goal each game is to win. Anything that happens from the start of the game until the final buzzer is just progress. This does not mean your team shouldn't celebrate when they score or feel anxiety when scored against—both situations can be great motivators. What I am saying is make sure your team acts like they have been in those situations before. Recognize if your team is constantly overzealous or discouraged with different situations. Treat that reaction as an alarm, an indicator that action needs to be taken to curb that behavior. This is something that should be a shared task between you, the other coaches, and the team leaders.

Finally, don't think this problem is limited to your players. As coaches, we also need to be in control of our emotions. We are all guilty of getting a little too excited or too discouraged on the sidelines once in a while. After all, we are human too. If you catch yourself doing this, compose yourself and then make sure to reinforce the right attitude immediately. As you go, the players will go—attitude reflects leadership.

Approach each new season like you are managing an entirely new team, even if your group is primarily populated by returning players. While a coach's dedication to his or her sport is at times all-consuming, one must not forget that life is still happening outside of the locker room, for everyone. Marriage, divorce, the loss of a family member, and the birth of a child, among many other happenings of life, are all things that can change a person at their core. For middle school and high school players, smaller events may also have a big emotional impact, so scale your gauge of this to accommodate that. It is because of this constant flux that you should adopt the idea that just because a tactic or way of teaching worked for one group does not automatically mean it will work for the next. Do not be afraid to challenge your own methods and question whether or not they will work with each team.

What to Do When It Happens

When you are in a slump, don't ignore it and hope for the best; I absolutely hate when teams do that.

Hope is death for an athlete.

It means you are unsure about yourself and your team, and you have decided to put your faith in another power. Your team's faith needs to be in each other, because together they create power.

During slumps, everyone involved tends to have a feeling of uncertainty in their minds and butterflies in their stomachs. This is because there are more questions than answers. The way to get out of this mental funk is to identify what these questions are and begin to search for the answers. If you know what's bothering you, it can be fixed.

Some common questions arise during slumps. "Why are we slumping?" "What do we fear as a team?" "How do we start scoring/winning again?" To find the answers to these questions, review what your team's mental approach was when you were winning and see what has changed. The answer to that can usually explain the reason the slump started in the first place.

Set Realistic Goals

In addition to answering the questions that are plaguing your team, you must also make sure that no unnecessary pressure is put on the team. Both players and coaches can be the culprit in this regard. For example, let's say your team is going through a losing streak. With every loss, the pressure to win builds. All of a sudden, before a regular season game, one of your players says, "This is a playoff game tonight. We *must* win." Most likely this teammate is just trying to motivate his or her peers, but statements like this can have traumatic effects if you don't win the game.

Try never to say to your team or the press that you "must" win the first half of a game or that you "must" get another player off their game, etc. If you then "lose" the first half of the game or you don't get the other player off their game, in your players' minds you have already lost the game. This is not a mental state you want your players in during a contest. Unless you will lose the entire game if you don't accomplish goals like these, don't set them. You want them to believe that no matter what the situation is, they are still in the game. In reality, the most effective message while going through a losing streak is, "This is just another competition. Relax and play your game."

During a slump, establishing goals and not ultimatums is imperative for your team. Even if far-fetched, goals give your group a tangible mission to accomplish whereas ultimatums create fear of losing. Creating a win-or-die atmosphere when one doesn't need to exist will inevitably set your team up for failure. The problem with fear is that most people don't ever want to talk about it. If fear is not addressed, it can morph into despair or worse. Remind your team to *never* fear failure, for it is an opportunity to better prepare you for adversity.

If your team loses sight of their communal goals, individual and selfish play can begin to infiltrate your team's performance. In addition, your players may begin to stray from game tactics that helped you find success earlier in the season. Keep reminding your players that your ability to play as a unit—especially during a slump—is how you have succeeded in the past, and it will continue to be the way to find success. Slumps are not a reflection on your entire season, just a fraction of it. Losing, especially a few times in a row, can help your team build resolve, mental discipline, and character—three things that will fortify the strength of your overall team bond.

Champions Have Slumps Too

Finally, when in a slump, do not be afraid to reference other great teams in the past that have gone through slumps but have still won championships. Besides the 1972 undefeated Miami Dolphins of the NFL, there are very few title-winning teams in any sport that did not hit a losing streak at some point during their championship campaign. This is why knowing how to handle lulls before they happen can be instrumental in helping your team break out of the lull and remain a competitor in the league.

Here is a list of a few championship teams that went through major slumps:

NHL:

2015–16 Pittsburgh Penguins (W-L-OT Loss)
- 0-3-0 to start the season
- 1-6-1 (five losses in a row) in December
- Result: WON Stanley Cup

2013–14 LA Kings (W-L-OT Loss)

- 1-4-0 streak in November

- Five-game losing streak late December into January

- Went 1-9-0 over ten games in January into February (five- and four-game losing streaks) and two three-game losing streaks during season

- Result: WON Stanley Cup

2008–09 Pittsburgh Penguins (W-L-OT Loss)

- 1-7-0 (five losses in a row) from December into January

- Three three-game losing streaks during the season

- Result: WON Conference and Stanley Cup

1990–91 Pittsburgh Penguins (W-L-Tie)

- Went 1-5-1 in October

- 2-9-1 in November into December

- 3-5-0 (three losses in a row) during first half of February, 0-4-1 in February into March

- Result: WON Division, Conference and Stanley Cup

1967–68 Montreal Canadiens (W-L-Tie)

- Went 2-6-3 (six winless) in October into November

- 0-5-3 November into December

- 0-3-1 February into March

- 0-3 to finish the season

- Result: WON Division and Stanley Cup (fourth of five in a row)

NFL:
2012 Baltimore Ravens

- Went 1-3 at end of the season
- Result: WON Super Bowl

2011 New York Giants
- 1-5 (four-game losing streak) during November into December
- Result: WON Super Bowl

2009 New Orleans Saints
- Went 0-3 at the end of the season after winning their first thirteen
- Result: WON Super Bowl

2005 Pittsburgh Steelers
- Went on three-game losing streak before winning last four
- Result WON Super Bowl

2001 New England Patriots
- 1-3 to start the season
- Result WON Super Bowl

NBA:
2010–11 Dallas Mavericks
- Six-game losing streak in January
- Four-game losing streak in April
- Result: WON NBA championship

2004–05 Miami Heat

- Four-game losing streak in December (started season 10-10)
- Three-game losing streak to end the season
- Six back-to-back loss games during the season
- Result: WON NBA championship

2003–04 Detroit Pistons

- 1-8 (six losses in a row) in February
- Result: WON NBA championship

1994–95 Houston Rockets

- Three-game losing streak in November
- Three-game losing streak in January
- Five-game losing streak in March
- Three-game losing streak to finish the season
- Result: WON NBA championship

1968–69 Boston Celtics

- Five-game losing streak in February
- Four three-game losing streaks throughout the season
- Result: WON ninth NBA Championship in ten seasons

MLB:
2016 Chicago Cubs

- Four-game losing streak in June
- 1-9 from June into July
- Had not won World Series since 1908
- Result: WON the World Series

2010 San Francisco Giants

- Four-game losing streak in April
- Five-game losing streak in May
- Seven-game losing streak in July
- Three back-to-back-to-back loss games during the season
- Result: WON the World Series

2002 Anaheim Angels

- Went 3-12 for the beginning of the season (six-game losing streak)
- Result: WON the World Series

2000 New York Yankees

- Lost last seven games of season
- Result: WON the World Series

1969 New York Mets

- 1-6 run in April (five losses in a row)
- Five-game losing streak in May
- Four-game losing streak in June
- Four-game losing streak in July
- Result: WON the World Series

Above all, the most powerful tool to helping your team get out of a slump is their bond to each other. When your players know they are going through hell together and they *can* come out the other side, this is often the catalyst to make sure they keep moving forward instead of taking a seat.

"If you're going through hell, keep going."

– attributed to Winson Churchill

This statement, which has been attributed to Winston Churchill and has been used in multiple variations, often includes an appropriate follow-up: "That's no place to stop."

COMMUNICATION

Great coaches tend to be great teachers. Great teachers tend to be great communicators. This means communication is the skill that coaches should work at as much as athletes need to work on their game. In both instances, the more experience one has, the better they will become.

When working in any group environment, personalities, priorities, and motivations will differ for each member of the team. The result of this is that we all learn in different ways. Some athletes can retain information just by hearing it, while others will not understand without seeing it in action or drawn on the board. In my experience, the best coaches (and staff) have an ability to convey points and teach the game in different ways. The collective ability of you and your staff to communicate information in numerous ways is essential to get the best from your players.

Finding the best methods to do this encompasses many aspects of your day-to-day operations. When and how you choose to speak to your team is paramount. For example, some coaches may run through drills minutes before a practice starts while others review hours ahead. Some coaches may use

> The best coaches (and staff) have an ability to convey points and teach the game in different ways.

a white board to show the drills while others may just vocally explain them. Who you choose to deliver the message to your team is also important. Some coaches allow their assistants to go over drills, while others take on the entire process themselves. There is no right or wrong way to communicate—however, finding the right mix for you and your team throughout the season is important.

After analyzing your team's current communication process, it might surprise you how many issues can stem from the lack of good communication.

IN THE LOCKER ROOM

Your locker room is a sacred place for your team. In that space, trust and accountability must be maintained at all times. In addition, having a clearly established hierarchy of how interaction between players and coaches should flow is essential to maintaining the stability of the group. When these elements exist, whether it be a serious or joking matter, everyone inside the team room should understand what is and isn't appropriate in regards to communication.

As the coach, you are the leader of this room, but you are not alone in running the room. Make sure that team leaders and assistant coaches also play a role in how communication is handled in this space throughout the year. Over the course of a season, whether it be ten games or one hundred games, the same speech or instructions by the same person can become repetitive. Don't be afraid to delegate the delivery of messages in your room. For example, one coach might be better at giving inspiring speeches to motivate your players before a big game, while another coach may be better at explaining drills in a way that receives maximum mental retention. Captains may be best suited to speak up in the locker room during gaps in play, while veterans may provide more one-on-one interaction. All of these roles are interchangeable—the key is to keep it fresh. For example, I have been part of teams where a different player is asked to read the starting lineup each game. On other teams, the coach would review practice plans with a different player each week and have that person deliver the drills to the team.

No matter what the message or the situation throughout the year, take the time to think about who may be the best person to share information so that your players will best absorb it. Even if you find something that works, don't be afraid to switch it up from time to time. A fresh voice can often break up the monotony of a season and keep your team's attention.

With all this said, the need to delegate different communicators is not an excuse one should use in order to avoid speaking because a situation is uncomfortable. It is inevitable that throughout the season there will be messages that no one will want to give. The speech after a tough loss or having to alert your team that someone has been traded, fired, or dropped from the team is never easy. It is your responsibility as leader and coach to deliver these difficult messages to your team.

PRACTICE

A lot goes into crafting practices. The process of planning and preparing drills for practice is time consuming. It involves juggling the aspects of teaching tactics and maintaining endurance while also keeping your team engaged—it is somewhat of an art and may be one of the most underappreciated parts of the job description. However, just like art, different people will have different views and understanding of what it is you are trying to accomplish.

No matter how obvious the point of a drill may seem to you, never assume your players will automatically understand. Putting together a great practice plan is half the battle. Your ability to make sure your players and staff understand and retain the lessons of that practice is the other half. Accomplishing this level of retention can be achieved through knowing how your players learn and by creating a routine to go over your practices that everyone can agree with.

For teams that I coach, I tend to go over practice drills with the players in a classroom situation an hour or more before practice. Doing this gives me time to properly explain the drills and allows the players time to ask questions if needed. It is a relaxed and, more importantly, an unrushed environment that is conducive for learning. If needed, I will hold this classroom outside of the actual locker room to give them a fresh setting with none of the common distractions. After we are done, I give the players some free time before asking them to get their gear on. Right before the actual practice begins, I will once again quickly run through the order of drills for that day.

When explaining drills, it is sometimes also beneficial to give each drill a clear and unique name. Doing this gives your players a better chance of remembering a drill when you call for it during practice. Saying, "We are going to run Drill Three" will not have the same lasting impact as, "We are going to run the 'Around the World' drill." This tactic works especially well for drills that you repeat throughout the season.

Also, be sure to empower your assistant coaches and team leaders by either sending them the practice plan beforehand or reviewing it with them prior to sharing with the team. If possible, hold a meeting with coaching staff and team leaders during the week to go over drills and ask for input. Doing this enables them to do their job in helping to keep players on track throughout the practice; it also follows the communication hierarchy you have developed and reinforces that. If an athlete gets lost during a drill, your assistant coach can pull them aside to make corrections, which is better than having to stop the drill altogether to explain. In short, the more people who know what's going on at practice, the smoother your practices will run.

Finally, make sure to have your practice plan printed out and posted in your locker room for players (and coaches) to reference. If you have the time, you can even email your practice plan to the players before they arrive. The more time your players have to review and retain drills, the better chance they have of executing them.

MOTIVATION

Do you know what motivates each player on your team? It's a good question. Perhaps the more important question is, "How can you inspire your players if you don't know what drives them?"

A common coaching mistake is assuming that players are (or should be) motivated in the same ways you are. In truth, there is no one correct way to motivate others. Some players are motivated by money, some by spending time with their family, and others simply by a passion for the game.

No matter where motivation is drawn from—as a leader, knowing what drives the people you work with will help you to get the absolute best from them. Discovering what motivates each person within the team and then knowing how to use that when communicating with your athletes is your greatest tool for inspiring results.

Finding out what motivates each of your players is not as hard as you think. It can be as simple as just asking them, "What motivates you to succeed?" The answers may surprise you. During your training camp or first few practices, in addition to one-on-one goal-setting, ask your players questions about what motivates and demotivates them.

> **How can you inspire your players if you don't know what drives them?**

In addition to being a powerful coaching tool for you, asking for this information also lets your players know you are committed to their best interests.

When you have concluded with the one-on-one meetings, compare and contrast the results with your coaching staff. Not only will you be able to see broadly what kind of motivation will work with your team, but you will be able to adapt your coaching style to achieve the absolute best results. Think of the benefits of knowing this before the season even starts!

As an example, during one of my coaching seasons, 95 percent of players on the team answered the question,

"What demotivates you?" with the same two answers: "losing" and "players who don't put the team first." These may sound like obvious responses, but this was the only time in my coaching career that almost an entire team answered that question the same way. This confirmed two things for the coaching staff: we had picked the team well and the players would commit to the team-first bonding mentality with ease. The result was a championship at the end of that season.

THE ELEPHANT IN THE ROOM

Interestingly enough when it comes to communication, the things that aren't said sometimes speak louder than words. While players range from quiet to outspoken, there are times during a season when no one wants to speak up out of fear of disrupting the team, causing a bigger problem, or just being wrong.

Perhaps there is a player in your room that speaks out of turn or makes condescending comments in a joking manner at inappropriate times. The team all smirks and chuckles, but it's clear that eyes are rolling at the same time. If this persists long enough, your player's narcissistic perception of their teammates may eventually begin to threaten the team bond. Even if this only causes the slightest hesitation during game play, it can be a problem.

Another example of an obvious problem that no one wants to discuss is when someone is constantly falling behind or not doing their job well. This can range from a player regularly showing up unprepared to equipment managers not having the team gear ready on time. At first it may be dismissed as a minor issue, but over time it can escalate into a very unneeded distraction for the team. While conditions like this don't always need immediate attention, make sure you are aware of the situation and monitor it closely so you can take action if needed.

If patterns like this emerge in your team's dynamic, use your judgment to determine the best course of action. If the problems of inappropriate comments or someone not doing their job worsen or consistently happen, it may be time to have a one-on-one with that player, or in some cases a "public" response from you that steers the conversation in the direction you prefer may be all that is needed. For some circumstances, a discussion with your coaching staff about any concerns you have with the individual's behavior primes them to be able to assist in gently communicating how the player can improve.

If you—or a member of your staff—feel that there may be an elephant in the room, address it sooner rather than later.

Approach your leaders and gauge their thoughts on what you are feeling. It may turn out that you are overthinking the situation, but you may find out that the situation has been bothering the group for some time. At the end of the day, squashing issues like this not only makes everyone feel better, but it can also save your team from unneeded internal pressure that can disrupt your group during an important part of the season.

At the end of the day, how you approach and discipline your team is up to you. These are just some suggestions to help prepare you. We all have our own personal stances on how to reprimand and correct our players. There is no one "correct" method. When problems like these occur, don't hesitate to consult your coaching staff and team leaders for their opinions in order to help you make the best choices.

THE DAMAGE AN ELEPHANT CAN DO

A year following my first collegiate championship as a player, we had a player on the team who was extremely talented as a hockey player but not talented as a student. Weeks into the season, he was already skipping classes and by midterms, he garnered a GPA below 1.0. In addition, he often would revel in the alcoholic excesses that college life provides.

Worst of all, he was allowed to play every game and in most cases was relied on during big plays throughout the first semester, even though he clearly did not meet the weekly academic requirements to play. The coach of the team was clearly ignoring his problems off the ice, to help the team on the ice. Several players on the team took exception to this. It was not uncommon to hear chatter between players along the lines of, "If he doesn't have to follow the rules, why should I?"

At the end of the term, the player was dismissed from the team for his lack of academic progress, but the damage was done. A lack of communication between the players and the coach, to make him aware of their disagreement with the situation—combined with the coach ignoring the situation outside the rink—caused a fracture in the team trust and bond that could not be fixed. In addition, the team's average GPA dropped steadily throughout the season.

Our team that season, that had won a championship the prior year, was knocked out in the first round. Had there been a better communication process in place for the players to voice their opinions, and had the coach listened to them or at least acknowledged the elephant in the room—and explained his thoughts on the situation—the team most likely would have been more successful. Instead, the problematic situation was left to fester for most of the season, thereby dooming the team to mediocrity.

CANCER 8

Have you ever heard the saying "That person is a cancer in the locker room"? When it comes to team building, a "cancer" is any individual or group that threatens your team bond by putting themselves above the collective goals and mission of the group. Many times when a cancer exists in your room, the focus is put on *who* is being attacked (another player, the coaching staff, the team as a whole, etc.) instead of *what* is being attacked. Understand that regardless of what it seems the cancer is attacking, the real threat is the destruction of your team bond.

Throughout the season, your team will face many threats—both as a group and as individuals. Injury and illness can come without warning. A losing streak can test your team's confidence to the breaking point. Player movement can shake up a team's chemistry. While these threats are all dangerous and can damage the team if not dealt with, they all take a backseat to the greatest threat any team will face. That threat is having a cancer in your room.

There are plenty of other terms that could have been used to describe this threat. I could have easily said, "that player (or behavior or attitude that the player has) is a disease" or "that player is a virus." So why do most coaches settle on using *cancer* as the term to describe a player that threatens the team?

Like cancer, different forms of the disease exist. Also like cancer, the disease can be easy to ignore or miss the warning signs that your team is in danger. For example, if you are winning consistently, it can be easy, or in some cases convenient, to miss the fact that the behavior of one or several of your players is starting to negatively affect the group.

Cancer is most deadly when it becomes invasive—when the disease (behavior, attitude) spreads from one player to others, the entire organism (team) is threatened. For example, winning and losing can both be a catalyst to bring out the best and worst in people. During a losing streak, it can become easy for players to question each other or the overall team strategy. Conversely, during a winning streak individual players may feel invincible, creating a false sense of confidence. If just one player begins to exude one of these messages or this behavior to the team, it can become highly infectious to the group. This is why whenever a streak is taking place, regardless of the variety, you need to be more focused on your team's emotional status and behaviors than ever.

As soon as you let your guard down, you leave yourself vulnerable to problems. Whether your team is going through good times, bad times, or is in the middle, always make sure you are aware of their emotional state and encourage them to remain focused and even-keeled. Complacency is the easiest way to allow cancer to sneak into the room.

Like cancer, once you realize there is a problem, treatment may need to be very aggressive and is not guaranteed to work.

For example, when you realize there is a disturbance in your room coming from a player or coach, you have to try to neutralize the threat by either speaking to or in some cases removing that person from the team. In addition to cleaning up whatever mess they made, there can be lingering questions and complications within your team that you will need to sort out and explain. For example, perhaps the player in question was a top performer or a favorite teammate to many in the room. Removing this person without an explanation will only cause resentment from your players instead of understanding. Make sure it is clear to your team what the player's actions were and why that is unacceptable and disrespectful to the organization. Some of the team may not have been aware of these actions. To be clear, when speaking to your team about the removal or punishment of a player, it does not need to be an open discussion where players can share their thoughts on the matter. However, it should be addressed in the room by the coaching staff in order to clear the air.

If you do not take the steps to make sure your team understands how a cancer threatens the group, you run the risk of allowing it to spread to other players. Moreover, if you wait too long to deal with a problem in your locker room, you run the risk of losing your players' trust and belief in what you are trying to accomplish. Once this happens, it is nearly impossible for the team's bond to survive, or to continue performing as a team and win.

The trick to avoiding all of these scenarios is prevention. Learn to recognize the signs that something is wrong and be prepared to deal with it. These can come in the form of something subtle like your athletes not looking you in the eye when you are speaking, to something severe like open insubordination from a player. As a coach, you are responsible for recognizing any growing threats within your group and take action.

Take the time to establish zero-tolerance rules and their punishments early in the season.

For example, have your players review and sign a player contract that establishes ground rules for the group to follow. For school teams this may be the understanding that a certain GPA is needed in order to dress, and for professional players it may be establishing punishments for show-ing up late or missing team meetings. In recent years, many teams have also implemented a strict "no phone or texting on game days" policy. Teams at all levels often have strict rules for players that run into trouble outside the team with law enforcement, typically regarding assault or DUI.

Work with your coaching staff and captains before the season to review what zero-tolerance rules will best help your team reduce the risk of defiance. Doing this will set the tone right from the start and define the standards you expect your players to follow. You can also delegate some of this responsibility to your team by letting them create ad-ditional rules for the locker room as well. Doing this type of "kangaroo court" (when players establish rules where their peers act as judge, jury, and executioner) gives your players ownership over the room and a sense of duty to follow their own rules.

The greatest tool in helping you detect cancer in the room is to establish a team bond.

The bond will automatically force your group to police them-selves and be accountable for each other throughout the season—because every player understands that what they do directly affects everyone on their team. When unity exists on your team, every player and staff member serves as a vital organ to its success. One failure can cause the entire body to shut down. When the integrity and accountability of players, coaches, and staff are linked together through an impenetrable bond, a team will simply not tolerate the presence of any internal or external threats.

TYPES OF CANCER

The first step to eradicating the team cancer is to educate yourself on recognizing the different types. This is done through both experience and trusting your instincts. If you feel something might be wrong, don't ignore it. Take the time to investigate.

Different coaches describe cancer in different ways. For some it comes in the form of players who disregard authority, either publicly or internally or both, which can destabilize your team's hierarchy. For others, it's in the form of athletes that selfishly drive attention to themselves and exclude their teammates from acknowledgment. Some forms of cancer can be easily detected and dealt with, while others can be subtle yet more deadly. No matter how they manifest, these cancers need to be identified and treated. This means identifying the player who is causing the problem and taking action, which can range from a one-on-one meeting to complete expulsion, in order to neutralize the threat they pose to the team.

SELF-SERVING BEHAVIOR

The most obvious type of cancer is a player who believes he or she is bigger than the team. This usually takes form in an athlete who is more focused on acquiring points or stats for self-gain and recognition over the team winning. Another common version of this is an athlete who doesn't give their best effort for selfish reasons. This can happen when a player is upset with their contract, has an option on the table to play somewhere else in the near future, or has a grievance with how they are being utilized by the coaching staff. While these are all realities of sport, a mature player will not let it affect their performance. It is up to you, the coach, to recognize players who are exhibiting this kind of behavior and take action to defuse the tension. This may mean taking the time to sit down with them one-on-one to work things out or, if the behavior continues, making the decision to take disciplinary action.

Disciplinary action up to and including termination should not be based on the player's ability but rather on that player's persona and ability to work with others.

Choosing to keep any player who is threatening your group's bond is akin to throwing gasoline on a fire—or feeding the cancer instead of treating it.

Doing so will not only cause your team to question their trust in you as a leader, but also their place on the team.

Staff Misconduct

Another type of cancer that is much more elusive comes from a staff member, in the form of anything from mistrust up to behavior that deliberately undermines your authority. For example, what happens if one of your assistant coaches is innocently sharing information with a player that was for the "coaches' ears only"? Or what if your assistant coach or athletic trainer is taking players out to meals and discussing what changes they would enact to make the team better— that you as the coach may not be doing? As coaches, we all know that players talk to one another outside of the room. It doesn't take much for an innocent coaching disagreement to be perceived as a full-fledged feud in your players' eyes. Any situation in which your athletes are led to believe there are cracks in your coaching staff can be catastrophic to your leadership ability.

Make a pact with your staff before the season starts that you will never purposely disagree or contradict each other in front of the team. It is completely normal for the members of your coaching staff to have different approaches to the game. In fact, the most successful coaching staffs usually have a good mix of differing personalities and tactics. However, shielding your players from coaches' business and disagreements is a necessity in order to maintain the team bond.

Whether on purpose or accidentally, any publicly aired disagreements will force your players to choose who is right or wrong. This can quickly split a team in half and shift their focus from executing the game plan to questioning the game plan. Always strive to appear as a unified front. As the head coach, do your best to identify when something

> Any publicly aired disagreements will force your players to choose who is right or wrong.

you say may contradict or inadvertently belittle one of your assistant coaches. At the same time, your assistant coaches should do everything within their power to avoid disagreeing or challenging you in front of the team. While this may happen by accident now and then, constant discord will only cause confusion and controversy within your room.

Hypocrisy

The deadliest type of cancer is also one of the hardest to detect. It comes in the form of head coaches who put their team in a position to question their integrity. Once you have set your expectations and established the team culture you want the group to live in, never—under any circumstances—compromise it by breaking your own rules.

These situations happen more often than you might think. Ever have an opportunity to bring in or sign a star player who will put up a lot of points, but who you also know is a horrible teammate? You'd be crazy if you didn't at least consider it, right? Or what if you knew that one of your assistant coaches, who is loved by the players, provided alcohol to underage players? As long as they don't get caught, no harm, no foul, right?

Temptations like these are everywhere and can occur throughout the season, for you as much as for the players. Playing a talent who constantly neglects the team rules and philosophy over a player who exhibits professionalism is one way to turn off your team. Appointing individuals whom your team does not respect into leadership roles due to favors or family affiliations is another way to lose the room. Any situation that causes your players to question their ability to trust you as their leader who will do what's best for the team is also a catalyst that will destroy the team bond.

Most coaches in this position believe they are doing what's best for the team. This is what makes this type of cancer so hard to detect. Regardless of perception, this is a case where your actions will speak louder than words. Falling victim to temptation and breaking your own rules is a quick way to lose the trust and respect of your team.

There are many signs that can indicate you might be losing your team's respect and faith. If players and staff repeatedly hint or suggest that you should change an aspect of your coaching style, do not dismiss it. It can be very easy for coaches to see these inferences as a challenge to authority or a lack of knowledge about the game, when in reality they are observations about yourself that may be hard to swallow. Always keep an open mind to every request and make sure that your team feels they are actually being heard.

Another indication that you may be losing your group's focus is their body language. When you speak, are they really listening and comprehending or just hearing and dismissing?

Additionally, are they looking you in the eye or is their mind somewhere else? If you start to see these signs, analyze what you are or aren't doing to engage your team and adapt your coaching style to best benefit your players.

HOW TO CURE CANCER

If the type of cancer you are dealing with is very small or isolated to one or a small group of players, it may be best to delegate the responsibility of dealing with it to a team leader or member of the coaching staff. While you should monitor all situations, trying to fix every issue that a team has will inevitably cause you to sacrifice focus from your other coaching responsibilities.

Choosing a delegate to work the problem is not only a vote of confidence from you, but also a message to your team that some problems do not need to immediately be escalated to the top. This can keep smaller incidents in perspective for your players and prevent them from growing into something larger in their minds. If the problem lingers or begins to escalate, then make the call to step in to help remedy the situation.

If a cancer begins to affect your entire team, take action immediately. Start by asking the player in question out for a one-on-one meeting to voice your concerns and clear the air. We all deal with stress in different ways. Sometimes giving a player the ability to get something off their chest or share their ideas can clear a problem.

If after speaking to a player the problem persists, more severe tactics such as suspension or expulsion from the team may be necessary. I suggest strongly that if you have a repeat offender you give them few, not many, opportunities to make things right before letting them go.

RECOVERY

If your team survives a bout with cancer, it does not mean the disease will never return. Always keep an eye out for resurgence. Moreover, cancer may leave your team in a weakened and vulnerable state. Recovery can take time and an incredible amount of patience.

If your players were aware of the problem you have dealt with, speak to them and discuss the actions that were taken. Although sometimes awkward and uncomfortable for your players, it will prevent the disease from festering and becoming worse. In addition to good communication, find ways to reinforce your bond through team-building practices such as team

> **If you have a repeat offender, give them few, not many, opportunities to make things right before letting them go.**

exercises or motivational speakers. Above all, make sure you and your team learn from the experience so that it will not happen again.

HOW REMOVING THE CANCER CAN HEAL THE BOND

No one else wanted my first job as a head coach. That collegiate team had finished the previous season in last place in their league and region. They had been on probation with both their school and their league for substance abuse, low GPAs, and other reasons, and the team faced uncertainty. Many thought it would be better to just do away with the program altogether. After speaking with the school about my plan to revitalize the club, the team was granted a one-year opportunity to turn the program around.

Prior to the end of the school year before I took over, I held a meeting with the returning players and made my vision and intentions very clear. I explained that in the coming season we would be taking a team-first stance—that this team would exemplify the meaning of the word teamwork and rise from its ashes the following season. In order to show me their dedication to these ideals, players were given a choice to meet me at 6:30 a.m. the next morning for a team workout, or be left off the squad for the following season.

The next morning, on a field covered in snow and with temperatures near freezing, every player showed up. I made it known that this event was meant to test their commitment to the program and they would have the summer to think about whether or not they would be willing to make the same commitment day-in and day-out next season.

Fast-forward to the fall and tryouts. It was made very clear that to make the team, all players would have to commit to a week-long training camp and tryout. Those not willing to make the commitment would be left off the team.

During the first two days of camp, one of the team's top players (and top troublemakers) from the year before did not show up. On the third day, he arrived with his gear and the excuse that he didn't feel he should have to try out for a team he had been the leading scorer on the year before.

I nodded and informed him that he knew that these try-outs were mandatory for all players and he would not be a member of the team for the coming season. After a brief and awkward silence, he turned around and walked out of the rink. That evening, I received an email from two of the players (numbers two and three in scoring, respectively) saying they would not be playing this season due to my dismissal of their friend.

Just like that, the top three scorers on the team were gone, and just like that the top three cancers were eradicated. Once word got around the team that these players were not going to be a part of the squad for the coming season, the mindset changed immediately.

In addition to establishing myself as the leader of the team, I also established that the team came before any one player, no matter how good they were. Although the team had a rocky start (we lost our first five games), they eventually found their footing and powered through the season for twenty-plus wins, a regional ranking, and one win away from making their league's national championship tournament. In addition, the team had the highest overall GPA average in the program's history.

Had I allowed the players who quit the team earlier in the season to stay, I firmly believe the team would have gone down the same path it had the year before. While their combined talent was remarkable, it led the team nowhere. At the same time, the average talent of our bonded team that first season led the team out of dire straits and back into prominence in the league. That first year, the team exemplified teamwork, heart, and an overall commitment to one another that set a foundation for the teams to come. And every person on the team learned a valuable lesson about what teamwork really is. It set the example of how creating the right mindset and establishing strong leadership can help to turn a program around. Within two seasons, the team made the national championship tournament (a presence they continued for many years), in addition to being nationally ranked.

FOCUS 9

When it comes to sports, the ability for your team and athletes to be even-keeled regardless of the situation is an ability that can make the difference between winning and losing. Achieving this type of mental stability is both an individual and a group practice. True balance on a sports team is the ability for athletes to clearly understand the parts of their lives they can control and to maintain focus on the present in order to create results. Simply put, when your team has the ability to focus only on what they can control, maximum results will be obtainable. Teams who don't have this ability will often lose their way and fall short.

THE CIRCLE OF CONTROL

No matter what sport you are involved in, there are going to be inevitable distractions throughout the year. From media coverage to general drama in the locker room, every day can breed new disruptions that detract from your team's ability to focus on the group and individual level. In reality, all distractions are relative, depending on how your mind processes them. Something that is perceived as a major dilemma for one person might be a ripple in the pond for another. Only when you and your athletes have an understanding of self-control and true perspective on what is important will the severity and number of issues your team must deal with diminish.

Every person has control of certain things in their life. We can control our physical actions (when we get up, when we eat, when we shower); we also control what we say and think. In addition to personal control, we all have levels of influence in daily life concerning how we deal with people and respond to different situations. Beyond these things, we have very little to no control over anything.

Realizing how little control you have over your life can make your world feel like a very small and confined space initially. However, upon reflection, you will find that the world is much larger than you think. I call this way of thinking the *circle of control*. It's a philosophy that in sports and life allows individuals to be mentally balanced, accountable, and focused. You do this by recognizing what you can control and releasing yourself from responsibility for and worry about those things you can't control.

The concept is simple: you live inside a circle with the things that you directly control. Outside of that circle is everything you cannot control. Worry only about the relationships, goals, and issues within your circle; spend time improving your behavior, accomplishments, and responses to problems, and don't worry about anything that is outside your circle. Responding to anything outside of your circle is a waste of time and energy.

Perhaps the best examples of this in sports are the match-ups each night other than your own team's. If you or your players spend time worrying about another team's results, you are wasting your energy. Moreover, if you constantly focus on the standings throughout the season or are worried about your placement, you are dedicating time and energy to something you can't control. As a team, you control how you perform each practice and each game.

If your team has the ability to truly focus 100 percent on their development, effort, and execution, the standings will take care of themselves.

The first step to adapt to this way of thinking is to identify exactly what you do control and influence. As a coach, you have direct control over the team selection, tactics, how you address your players, and many other aspects of the day-to-day operations of the team. However, no matter how much you would like it, you have no direct control over how your athletes play on any given day. You have no direct control over the choices they make away from the team in their own time. You have no direct control over their personal thoughts.

Learning to decipher what you can control and then focusing only on those matters is not an easily achieved mindset. It can be even harder to identify the aspects that you can't control. In truth, you control very little in this world beyond your own actions, yet most people spend time worrying about what they don't control. Only when you see what is inside your circle of control will you be prepared to take on the curveballs that life and sports can throw at you. True mastery of this is only achieved with patience, resolve, and experience.

Think about how this applies to sports. It is very easy for players to get lost worrying about the things they don't control. Bad calls from the officials, fan reaction, press reports, and the performance of other teams—among many other distractions—are all examples of things outside of their circle. Players who understand what they do and do not control will be in a position to give maximum focus to their craft and not waste any energy on distractions.

Coach your players to explore and understand this concept. Explain to them that their preparation and performance, how they conduct themselves in public and private, and what kind of teammate they are—among many other things—

are all things they directly regulate. This can be explained through one-on-one and group meetings and also metaphorically through team exercises.

As an example, one of the physical challenges I have my team put through early in the season is small-group raft building. In groups of four, players are given four large barrels, two legs of rope, and four pieces of plywood. They are then instructed that they have fifteen minutes to build a raft out of these materials and then they will have to race. When the clock starts, teams frantically begin to concoct a plan. Usually about five minutes in, we start to see some teams look and review how other teams are building their rafts. Sometimes if another group looks further along, we see other teams change their game plan to match. Nine times out of ten the teams that copy each other end up sinking. The group that tends to win this competition is the one that stays focused on their project and their group's ideas without wasting any time focusing on what other teams are doing and how far along they are. The lesson is that the time you spend focusing on what you don't control, no matter how attractive it may be, is a waste. Only the team that focuses on their own resources and how best to utilize them finds success in this exercise.

When this type of thinking is applied to your locker room, an entirely new level of team focus is possible. This will give way to many other concepts that can benefit your team throughout the year.

LIVE IN THE NOW

It can be easy for anyone to get lost reliving the past or daydreaming toward the future. While a level of reflection and projection is healthy in order to learn and set goals, too much can hinder your ability to take action in the present. The "present" can be looked at in several ways. In some instances, it is quantified as this month or week, while for others it's simply today. While both of these definitions apply to sports, during games the present literally becomes a second-by-second focus. This is why, no matter whether a situation is good or bad, I always tell my players to "live in the now."

Players and coaches can easily lose focus by dwelling on a recent mistake made just minutes ago. We see this play out in baseball with pitchers all the time. As the pitch count goes up, so does the stress on a pitcher's arm. One bad at-bat can easily turn into two, and very quickly a pitcher can find himself with the bases loaded.

Conversely, players and coaches can also be guilty of thinking a game is won when there is still time left on the clock. We see this play out in basketball, in the final seconds of a one-point game. One team makes what they think is the winning shot with just a few seconds left, and do not aggressively get back on defense—allowing the other team to sneak in a last-second basket to steal the victory back.

No matter what the situation is, the ability to recognize that your team is not focused on what is playing out in front of them and coaching them on how to focus in the now can make the difference between winning and losing the game.

This mental toughness is very important in high-pressure situations, such as overtime or playoff elimination games. When a game or your season is on the line, it can seem that every single play has more importance than normal. In these amplified situations, your team's ability to control their emotions is imperative. These are the moments where self-control and an ability to focus on what is in front of them will help them perform to their potential and keep players from being paralyzed by the situation.

Teams that are used to winning can grow an unhealthy fear of losing.

When teams in this position finally lose, the failure can cause a dreadful doubt that reverberates in the locker room and can put even the best teams into a tailspin. These groups tend to get stuck in the moment and dwell on the result rather than moving past it.

Teams that are used to losing can be afraid to win. This tends to show itself with squads that consistently blow leads late in games. Teams in this position are gripped by the premonition that they will blow a lead, leaving them focused on not losing instead of focusing on winning. Both of these situations demonstrate a team's inability to live in the now.

This thinking can also be applied to the season as a whole. It can be easy during a losing streak to focus on what things were like prior and also begin to fantasize toward the near future when the losing will end. During a winning streak, it can be easy to feel complacent and therefore be vulnerable to losing. You can only achieve true mental balance when you focus on what is happening

The same focus works under all circumstances and will help everyone perform at their best—whether you won or lost, just scored, or made a critical error.

in the present. The real truth here is that the same focus works under all circumstances and will help you and the team perform at your best—whether you won or lost the last match, and whether your team just scored or made a critical error.

The practice of "focusing on the now" is essential to finding balance both in life and in sports. We cannot change our last action any more than we can predict the future. Teams that are truly able to stay in the moment mentally and emotionally will have the best chance of staying even-keeled and succeeding.

PLAYBOOK 10

Throughout this book, we have discussed the key elements needed to create a team bond. While explaining these concepts to your staff and team is a good starting point to help build a strong understanding of the ideal, nothing beats practice to instill these habits.

There are many metaphorical and physical ways to help your group fully comprehend the importance of the bond to winning. In this chapter, we will review different tactics and techniques that you can provide to your team in order to help build, fortify, and nurture an impenetrable team bond throughout the season.

By far one of the best tools that you and your team have at your disposal is the Internet. It has never been easier to research and find information and videos that you can share with your team. In addition, the ability for you to communicate this information to your players through email and other digital means allows you to be more proactive than ever before as a coach. Coaches who learn and utilize this technology to the fullest will have an advantage over the competition.

TRAINING CAMP

Creating a strong training camp to begin your season is the most critical step in establishing your bond. A training camp can be a one-day or a weeklong event prior to the start of the season, encompassing drills, classroom sessions, and meetings with your team in a secluded setting. It is your opportunity to establish the foundation for a team bond in addition to setting goals both individually and as a group.

Typically when running a training camp, I hold a brief meeting for introductions and to address the players on the exact reasons for the camp. I say that during our time here we will set a foundation for a team bond and implement it through team-building exercises in order to grow into a team that will win championships. Some coaches and players don't like to actually say "championship" so early in the season. I don't agree with this thinking. I want my players to always know what it is we are going after from day one.

Just like drills at practice, when an athlete comprehends the purpose of a drill at camp and how it applies to the game, there is a much better chance they will understand its significance. All of the drills, meetings, and classroom sessions that are part of a training camp should have a very specific meaning and purpose. Some of these meanings might be presented prior to starting the drill while others should be allowed to reveal themselves over the course of the exercise. No matter which approach you are taking, the "team, teammates, self" priority philosophy should always be the basis for all activities.

I am always amazed at how fast teams come together over the course of a training camp.

Sometimes the subtlest aspects of a camp are the most telling. For example, many times at the training camp's first meal, players tend to spread themselves out in the cafeteria or eating area. By the last day, without fail, the entire team is sitting together in the same area.

When you ask your players to go through this experience together, it sets the foundation right away that the only way to succeed is to work together. Instead of players focusing on positions and placement to start the season, they are instead motivated to work at surviving the training camp together.

This aspect alone will give your team a head start on the competition for the season. For an example training camp schedule, see the bonus material at the end of the book.

IN-SEASON TEAM-BUILDING SESSIONS

While a training camp will give your team a major boost to start the season, it is also important to hold team-building sessions throughout the year. These drills should be used as a way to reinforce or remind your players of the foundations that the season is based on. Many factors can unbalance a team and knock players off this path—losing streaks, winning streaks, trouble in the locker room, or even just the monotony at some point in the season.

The key factor when planning in-season team-building exercises is timing. This is a tactic that should be used only when needed and not "just because." Every sports season has several predictable rough spots. For example during winter sports, late December and early January are usually very busy times outside of your team. As this point usually hits two to four months into a season, it is common for players to hit a bit of a wall from the general weekly grind in addition to wanting to spend time with their families. You can prepare or restore your players mentally with a training exercise prior to or after this time to fortify the mindset you want your team to exhibit moving forward. Other key times where training sessions are a good idea are mid-season, prior to a playoff push, prior to a playoff run, and between playoff rounds/games. A moral boost during all these times can give your group an advantage over the competition.

In addition to choosing the right time, you must also choose the right activity. For example, if you feel there is a lack of trust in your locker room due to a minor player disagreement, make sure you choose an exercise that reinforces your athletes' dependence on each other in order to succeed. Simply doing a drill that emphasizes the importance of team play will not have the effect you are looking for. Make sure to fully understand the mental state of your group and create a session that will maximize their ability to work together.

ONE-ON-ONE AND SMALL GROUP MEETINGS

Although we strive to create a singular mission and foundation for the entire team, at the end of the day your players are still individuals. Plan to have one-on-one meetings with the players at least twice throughout the season to both review progress and discuss any issues that are on their minds—or yours.

When on a team, it can be very common for players to feel that, as individuals, they are not being heard. Reassuring your athletes that they have a voice, regardless of their role, will help to continually get the best out of them throughout the season.

These meetings can also help you to uncover things that are bothering your team as a whole that you might not have been aware of. The one-on-one setting allows players to speak freely about things that may be bothering them that they might not be comfortable discussing in front of the team.

Better to be surprised by this in these meetings, so you can assess if it is a threat before it actually becomes one.

In addition to one-on-one meetings, also hold get-togethers with small groups of players. This could be divided by position, team role, or however you see fit. Creating small teams within the team can help bring additional focus to the tasks you have for the members of a small group. It can also create healthy competition among groups, which can create even more focus. For example if you challenge your defense to have the lowest goals/points against the average in the league and your offense to have the most goals/points in the league, both groups will strive to reach their goal faster than the other. This can produce some amazing results if directed correctly.

MOTIVATIONAL VIDEOS/AUDIO

This is one of the most underrated techniques to get the best out of your team before a big game. Athletes are emotional beings. The ability for them to harness that emotion and focus it in a way to enhance performance is a very valuable tool for both the individual and the team. While I say several times in this book that staying even-keeled is the best mentality to find success, there is nothing wrong with providing your team with a healthy mental boost before the game starts. Even-keeled does not mean they aren't experiencing emotions—it means they are keeping their emotions in check so they don't lose sight of team goals or lose focus on the "now."

Creating or finding the right motivational video for your team is a process that requires creativity and research. I find the best type of motivational videos are two to four minutes long and include footage of your players and highlights from your games, a very clear message or speech, and the right music track. When these aspects are mixed together, a video can create a very focused tone that will heighten your athletes' hunger and senses prior to the start of a game. If done right, the benefits can be remarkable and sometimes astonishing. This approach can also be used to communicate a message that would not be effective if you just tell them.

The best way to start building a motivational video is to search YouTube for videos that have a specific message that you are trying to convey. You will be surprised by how many are out there. Take the time to look and find a few that motivate you, as odds are they will also motivate your team. Once you find one, you can download the video and overlay your own footage on top.

For example, prior to each game of a single-elimination play-off series—our first together as a team that would eventually win a championship—I mixed footage of our game play along with some cinematic shots of the players from our team media day with a speech that Al Pacino's character (who was a professional football coach) gave before a big game in the movie *Any Given Sunday*. The result of showing this was a four-goal lead after the first period (including one less than a minute into the game). For the following game, in which we were matched against the highest scoring and top-ranked team in the league, we created a new video to show the team. The result was a 4-2 victory in which we never trailed the opposition. For the next and final game, we created one last video that set the tone for a 5-3 win and championship for our team. Again, the team never trailed the opposition.

Once again, the most important aspect to keep in mind when deciding whether or not to use this tactic is timing. Showing your team an incredibly inspirational video days out from a big game is a waste. All you will do is rile them up, only to have that feeling deflate in the days before the game. I find the optimal time to play an inspirational video for your team is literally right before they need to leave the locker room for the start of the game. When using this tactic with teams, I will time out how long the video is and start playing it when we have just over that much time on the clock before going out. For example if a video is two minutes long, I will start it two minutes and thirty seconds before we need to leave the room.

The best time to use motivational videos is before games of extreme significance like playoff games or trophy-clinching situations. This technique can also be used if you are trying to jump-start your team out of a losing streak. However, be careful with this option. If the video does not work, you will lose your ability to use it the rest of the season. Once the tactic is associated with a loss it is very hard to regain its ability to motivate your team with the same emphasis again.

If you don't feel comfortable searching and creating these types of videos, ask to work with your team's media team or your campus' broadcasting department, or equivalent. If time is of the essence, you can also just choose an existing video from the Web to share with your team. No matter where you coach or what your budget is, there are always opportunities to follow through with this tactic.

QUOTES AND SAYINGS THROUGHOUT THE YEAR

Sometimes finding the right words to convey a message to your team can best be done by using someone else's. The best part is there are nearly an infinite number of quotes and images you can borrow from. Websites like brainyquote.com or just a general google search will give you access to millions.

Don't feel you need to limit yourself to quotes from people just involved in your sport. Good quotes can come from any-where. Sometimes I find quotes from athletes who were prominent in sports other than my own, and other times I find quotes from former military leaders, politicians, and influential authors.

Sharing these quotes with your team at the end of an email, on the wall of the locker room, or during a speech is an easy way to shake up the monotony. How often you use this technique is up to you. I have been on some teams where the coach would send a quote a week to his players and others where quotes were used sparingly but effectively throughout the year.

GUEST SPEAKERS

If you want to literally use someone else's words to help get a point across, bring in a guest speaker to your locker room. I actually believe this to be an important tactic throughout the year. No matter what sport you are involved with, the same voice in the locker room over and over again throughout the year can lose its emphasis if you don't shake things up.

Guest speakers can range from past players and legends from your program, to military heroes, to other motivational individuals. It all depends on the type of message you are trying to give your team.

For example, a collegiate team I was involved with was heading into a playoff game. After asking our current captain's permission, I invited the previous year's captain (who had graduated the year before and was loved by the players) to come into the room to give the guys a boost before the game. The move supercharged the team into a strong start and victory. Both the knowledge that their former captain had come back to support them and the excitement he showed to be there helped clear any doubt from our players' minds.

Another way to use this tactic is to give your players some perspective. I often invite military members to speak to my groups in order to share how important teamwork, communication, leadership, and other ideals are to helping the armed forces accomplish their missions. Not only do the players leave with a tremendous feeling of respect for those individuals and their duty, but they apply it to their own game. It's a humbling experience that puts into perspective how lucky they are to be playing the sport they love while others defend their freedom to do so. Moreover, it supports the attitude that to not give 100 percent would be to let down those who give all to serve.

Just like team-building exercises, timing with this tactic is very important. Don't randomly bring in a speaker just to do it. This can work against you, especially if you do it too much. Your voice must remain the top authority in the room. Speakers are best during a training camp, before big games, or to help motivate your team if they are stuck in a slump. Regardless of the reason you want a speaker, make sure you vet anyone coming into your room and make sure to discuss the message you are hoping they will get across to your team. Make sure that it does not contradict the foundations you have built for the season.

TRIPS TO LOCAL SCHOOLS/EVENTS

Helping to establish a locational identity for your team is an important aspect of building a team bond. Get your group out of the locker room and away from the arena, court, or field every once in a while to allow them to interact with fans, kids, and others in the community. The change of scenery will do them good.

In addition to a difference in venue, it will help to remind your athletes that the team is more than just the group playing the games. Interacting with the local community can help develop a selfless attitude within your locker room. While people outside of the team should have no effect on the way your team plays the game, knowing that they support and love the organization can be a strong source of motivation throughout the year.

In addition, community outreach is also a great way to encourage your players to adapt the mindset that the team is much bigger than them. Sometimes knowing that you can have a positive impact away from the game can in turn inspire you to have a positive impact in the game.

PLAYBOOK

No matter what sport you coach, you should make a playbook for your athletes. Traditionally, playbooks hold "X" and "O" tactics and systems that you will deploy throughout the year. Depending on the sport you coach, this might be a lot of plays or just a few. This is usually the deciding factor for most coaches on whether or not a playbook is actually worth their time.

There are many other tactics outside Xs and Os that you use during the year. Mental strategies, physical fitness and training techniques, public appearance guidelines, and many other aspects of the way you run your team are tactics that you should include.

CLASSROOM SESSIONS

In addition to the common pre-practice and pregame talks that you have with your team, also provide classroom sessions throughout the year to go more in depth into strategies and give your team the opportunity to ask questions.

These types of sessions can range from literal whiteboard tactical talks to a game video review. As coaches, we are often so engrossed in planning and preparing tactics that we can easily make the mistake of thinking the players are on the same page. Here is a good rule of thumb: every hour you spend preparing for the week should equate to ten minutes of classroom for your players. Depending on how much time you prepare, this might mean daily classrooms or just weekly.

When doing a classroom session, sometimes it can be beneficial to do it outside the locker room. Depending on your facilities, a classroom or lounge may be a better environment than the locker room. This will allow your players to be in a much more relaxed mindset that is more conducive to learning instead of preparing to do battle.

Both drawing plays and tactics and showing video are very powerful tools for your team. Regardless of which you use, make sure your classroom does not turn into a lecture. Encourage your players to volunteer the answers and ask questions in order to better understand the content. This will give them both confidence and ownership over what you are trying to accomplish.

When using video it is also important to show both negative and positive situations from games. This will help your players to understand they need to get rid of bad patterns and continue with good habits. You want your players to leave a classroom setting feeling encouraged and not discouraged.

TRY NEW THINGS

The above are just some of the methods I have found to be successful during my time as a coach.

Your ability to take these ideas and make them your own is what will make them successful for you and your team.

Coaching is always an evolving art, and at the end of the day, we need to learn from each other in order to expand our understanding of how to best manage teams.

Always keep an eye out for new ways to show players how important the bond is and how to advance their play to the next level. Bring your coaching staff in on the mission to develop new approaches, drills, and team-building activities. Make a habit of periodically introducing experimental exercises and gauge how your players respond. Sometimes a variation on an existing favorite will help everyone, including you as the coach, learn something new.

Above all, make sure you believe fully in any team-building tactic you implement with your team. Most players have a sense of when you are being authentic with your approach and when you are reaching. You don't have to fully understand an idea, but you do need to completely believe in a concept before using it with your team. This is why it's so important to surround yourself with a great support staff.

THE BOND IS THE BEGINNING OF SUCCESS

When a team is successful, a unique feeling reveals itself. It's very hard to describe but I believe the only thing it can be compared with is the brotherhood that soldiers feel in battle. When it is present and felt by both coaches and players, things are going the right direction. It manifests itself in a unified excitement to show up to practice and games each day. It's an understanding that, no matter one's personal thoughts of another teammate, they can trust that person. It's knowing that every person in the locker room plays for the success of their team and teammates before their own. This feeling is the presence of a team bond. If you don't feel this when coming to work each day, strive to find or create it. You cannot win without it.

Coaching is as much a calling as it is a privilege. There are many who try it but few who succeed. Those who succeed understand that the position of "coach" encompasses more than tactics and talking. As a coach, you are a teacher, mentor, motivator, and leader of young men and/or women. You are, for all purposes, the head of a family. It is a selfless and relentless journey that requires a tremendous amount of sacrifice and self-control. Surround yourself with the people and players who are also willing to take the journey and you will succeed.

ON WINNING AGAIN

Once the champagne was all gone and the inevitable after-parties and team awards night had concluded, the season officially came to an end. For the moment, the players could enjoy being champions in what many refer to as the "endless summer."

However, for the coaching staff, the end of the season is not endless—it just means the start of another. As the cool spring weather gave way to summer heat, our staff was right back to work planning our follow-up campaign. We knew the stakes would be even higher in the coming season and that we had become a "team to beat" in the league. And so the grind began again . . .

AFTER THE WIN

Winning affects everyone differently. For some it serves as validation and for others redemption. At the same time, for some it can allow time for an overdue vacation, while for others it serves as motivation to work even harder during the off-season. No matter how you view this period, do not let victory defeat you. Make sure you have plans in place for both

> **Do not let victory defeat you.**

your players and coaching staff for the off-season so that you can be prepared for the following season.

There is a reason we kept the word "season" in "off-season," it's because it's not a vacation— it's just the time of year where games aren't played. Being a coach is a full-time, year-round cycle. When one season ends, another begins.

A very common mistake that coaches make after winning is to relax. While it is absolutely a good idea to take some time off after each season to regroup and recharge (and revel in victory if that's the case), if you are not careful, what should be a two- to three-week vacation can easily turn into a two- to three-month break. As coaches we all have a fire inside that burns and keeps urging us toward victory. You can allow winning to either extinguish the flame or stoke your fire even more.

KEEP THE FIRE BURNING

Creating a championship culture is an art.
Building a team that wins consistently over time
is the masterpiece all coaches strive for.

In order to accomplish this, the same types of team goals and bonding exercises used to create the bond must become a shared mission for your entire organization, to maintain that bond. This shared mission and attitude toward winning must permeate everything and everyone from the owner(s), to the general manager, to the coaching staff, to the team, and the game-night staff.

In reality, sports organizations are a team in and of themselves. In order for the business to succeed, everyone, regardless of how large or small their role may be within the organization, must share ideals of trust, identity, communication, accountability, and leadership.

Organizations should also hire employees who are willing to buy into the group vision and culture.

As an example, when visiting what would become NASA's Kennedy Space Center in 1962, President John F. Kennedy stopped the tour he was being given after noticing a janitor in the hall with a broom. He walked over to the man, introduced himself and asked, "What are you doing?" The janitor responded, "Well Mr. President, I'm helping to put a man on the moon." Seven years later, that goal was accomplished.

This brief but inspirational story is a perfect example of a team that had established clear goals and an overall mission that included everyone—and even the janitor had bought into it fully. In order to win, there are no small roles; everyone plays a part toward victory. Building this type of belief and commitment throughout an organization is everything.

THE EVOLUTION OF THE BOND

In addition to the organization as a whole, your ability to take team-building concepts and evolve them within your own coaching style to produce a fresh environment each season is one of many factors that will help you and your team maintain a championship caliber over time.

It is very important to realize that every team you coach, no matter how many returning players or staff members from the previous season, is different. The tactics you use to build a bond and motivate your group one year may need to be completely different the following year.

One of the exercises I like to run through each off-season, in addition to reviewing the overall team's performance, is to review all the team-building tactics used the year before and then challenge myself to either find a different or better way to implement them the following season. It starts with training camp and continues all the way through how we choose to motivate players for the playoffs.

As each team is different, each season should mean new slogans, goal-setting sessions, and team-building events. Take the time during the off-season to discuss new approaches with your coaching staff and returning captains.

For players, the off-season is an opportunity to work on their individual games and athleticism without the rigors of the season. For coaches, the off-season is an opportunity to work on improving through education. Take the time while you can to research other coaching methods and approaches to the game. Just like your athletes, you should always be looking to expand your skill sets and improve your understating of your sport.

As coaches, building a strong trust and relationship with your players is essential to finding success—however, you cannot ever allow those relationships to cloud your judgment toward what is best for the entire team. Your ability to coach athletes is not based on just the current relationships you have with players, but your ability to continue to build and maintain relationships with all of your players, new and returning. No matter how close you are with any player or coach within your room, the team and organization must always come first. Do not allow your personal feelings toward any member of your squad to compromise that.

No matter what level you coach, player movement is inevitable—whether caused by graduation or free-agency status. Moreover, the players who fill in the gaps may or may not be selected by you, depending on what level you coach. It's important to realize that while there are players on your team whose contributions on and off the field of play are invaluable, the truth is most athletes are interchangeable. Whether a member of the team is departing your team or arriving, always approach the situation with class and understanding.

Successful organizations know there must be a strong core of top talent and leadership. However, they also know that in order to compete continually the roster must consistently be replenished. Teams must be willing to part ways with certain players no matter how impactful or influential they were in previous seasons, depending on the value they bring to the team currently. This is not to say that you should blindly dump a franchise player who has put in his time or a top draft pick or recruit whose skills have waned, but you should never find yourself in a position to say, "We can't move this person because of what they did for the team in seasons past." That's not fair to the organization or the team itself. Any player who no longer holds value toward the goal of winning should be expendable.

WIN AND WALK TOGETHER FOREVER

The journey your team takes together is the gift of the entire experience—don't forget to embrace it!

No matter what your end goal is as a team, the journey is the most important part. The golden moment of victory, while memorable, is just a blink in terms of the overall quest. Regardless of the end result, make sure your group knows to embrace all moments from the trip, good and bad, for they will define the experience more so than any trophy or accolade won.

Fred Shero, head coach of the Philadelphia Flyers' 1974 and 1975 Stanley Cup teams, told his players before taking the ice in the game that would see them win their first championship, "Win today and walk together forever." This short saying sums up the benefit of team bonds perfectly. Not only do those Stanley Cup teams live in Philadelphia sports lore, but also a majority of the team stayed in the Philadelphia area after their careers and made it their home. They embodied the quote figuratively and literally.

Creating a team bond is about creating relationships. When I look back at my professional experiences, whether it is in sports or in an office, the brightest memories were of being part of a team and what we accomplished together. I have come to understand the importance of those relationships and shared experiences—because the majority of people I stay close with today were part of those teams. The bond that existed then still exists today.

> **Win today and walk together forever.**

Tactics and talent fade in time but the bond stays strong—that's power that is worth investing in.

TO THE VICTOR GO THE SPOILS

We've all heard the saying, "To the victor go the spoils." For some that means trophies and other silverware to be displayed on a mantle or in a room with other accolades. For others, it means the excesses of fame, fortune, and notoriety. By far, the thing that I cherish most about winning—aside from the overall experience—is the team championship photo.

If you were to walk into my office right now, you would see no trophies or awards. What you would see is a wall of team championship photos. Cherished moments frozen in time, of a group huddled together screaming at the camera, with their hands signaling that we are number one. These photos are worth more to me than any trophy. The photo represents a moment of complete joy and accomplishment as a group. It represents the power of the team bond.

A trophy's shine and fame will fade over time, but for some reason, championship photos only get brighter.

BONUS MATERIAL:

PRESEASON TRAINING CAMP ITINERARY

The following itinerary is an example of the type of program I have used with multiple teams to build a strong foundation for the team bond and a winning season. Feel free to adopt this program for your own needs; it works as well for other sports as it has for hockey.

Welcome to *Your Team Name.* . .

The following document outlines our plan to maximize our team's championship foundation built on the bond of our players and coaching staff. In order to fortify this bond, we have prepared a two-week training camp. Included in that camp will be an overnight trip with the team that will incorporate a mix of new **team-building** exercises and activities, **classroom** environments in which we will establish an understanding of what kind of hockey team we will be this season, and **identity-building** events to help us establish our identity for the upcoming season. Following the overnight event, we will use the following week and a half to work on the ice and in preseason games to prepare ourselves for the regular season.

In addition to our team bond, another reason we continue to compete at a high level is our dedication to a circle of trust that is explained on the next page. Finally, we will continue to embrace and build upon our ideals of **accountability, winning and losing as a team, playing 60-minute hockey,** and understanding the prioritization system of **team, teammates, and self.**

Above all, we must display the **mental discipline** of a championship team. This encompasses everything from showing up early to team meetings and functions to taking the extra time to ask questions and educate yourself to become the best hockey player you can be for the team.

Over the past two seasons the *Team Name* has re-emerged as one of the top teams in the *League Name*—we intend to remain in that role. Each one of you was handpicked for this team because we believe that you understand and will commit to the ideals listed above and throughout this packet. For this season, your ability to commit both as individuals and as a team toward our common goals will drive us to victory.

Let's get to work!

The Coaching Staff

"Where there is unity, there is always victory."

– Publilius Syrus

CIRCLE OF TRUST AND ORDER OF COMMUNICATION

To be a *Team Name* is to commit to maintaining a circle of trust between the coaching staff, captains, players, and selected managers. Within this circle is where our team bond lives. No member within the circle may ever break the trust of another member. Any cracks or bends within can cause the entire bond to break.

Once it is established who is in the circle of trust, an order of communication must be maintained. While all members of the circle are free to talk to each other, when there is need to follow a chain of command, the below order should be kept in order to avoid miscommunication and other problems. No breaks in this chain should be tolerated.

HEAD COACH
↕
ASSISTANT COACHES
↕
CAPTAINS
↕
PLAYERS

TEAM SLOGANS AND PHOTOS

The below slogans are recurring messages that are displayed in our locker room all season long. They represent both our expectations and priorities for this season. More may be added throughout the year.

Sixty Minutes!

The hardest thing to do in the game is play a full 60-minute game at one's full potential. Players on this team strive for this every game for the entire season.

Team, Teammates, Self

The order that Team Name players and coaches must prioritize.

Accountability

We win and lose as a team. Every coach and player accepts the responsibility that how we perform (winning, losing, or in between) is done so as a team, not as individuals. We must surround each other in times of despair as well as times of triumph.

Team Photos

Within our locker room are several team photos from championships and training camps of the past. These should serve as a reminder that the *Team Name* organization spans several decades. As part of this team, you will help to build from our past and secure a legacy moving forward. Our goal should be to have our own photo on the wall for future teams to reference.

ESTABLISHING TEAM IDENTITY

Along with our team messages, it is also important that we establish an identity. When building an identity, we are giving ourselves a solid foundation on which to base our play. The question should never be asked, "What are we playing for?" yet the answer should always be obvious.

Below are some activities that we hope to accomplish during training camp.

Unity Piece – Players will decide on and find or create some object that signifies the ideals we are striving for as a team so that it can be awarded within the locker room to a player each game that best portrayed those principles. The player awarding the item will be the previous game's winner.

Team History – Can you name all the team's retired numbers? Our organization is bigger than any one player. As a member of this organization, you represent its history and all the players of the past—make sure you know it.

***City/School* History** – How much do you know about the city you play for? Through several methods, the history of our *city/school* and the surrounding areas will be taught to the coaching staff and team.

Fan Conduct – Regardless of their overall knowledge, or lack of knowledge, when it comes to hockey—without the fans, we would not have a team. During training camp, all players will be required to attend a brief media training seminar that will help to optimize their ability to interact with our fan base. All players will be expected to make personal appearances this season.

TEAM ACCOUNTABILITY

In order to create team accountability, we must establish both common and individual goals. To do this, you will be required to go through a goal-setting session with members of the coaching staff as well as a group goal-setting session.

Some of the individual questions you may be asked are:

- How many points do you see yourself scoring this season?
- What will (could) keep you from accomplishing your goals this season?
- What are your strengths as a hockey player?
- What are your weaknesses as a hockey player?
- How can you improve as a hockey player?
- How will you contribute to the team outside of point production?

- What motivates you?

- What demotivates you?

- Why did you choose to play for City/Organization Name?

- How can we help you achieve your goals this season?

Some of the team questions you may be asked are below:

- Where do you think we can/want to finish this season?

- What are our strengths as a team?

- What are our weaknesses as a team?

- What can we do as a team to improve?

- How do we define success as a team?

- What can keep us from accomplishing our goals?

TEAM NAME TRAINING
CAMP/PRESEASON SCHEDULE

Week 1

Day 1

12:30 PM – Meet at rink

12:45 PM – Drive to camp site

1:00 PM – Arrive at camp site

1:30 PM – Team meeting

2:30 PM – Team workout #1

4:00 PM – Walk to water area

4:30 PM – Team workout #2

6:30 PM – Break

7:30 PM – Team dinner

8:30 PM – *Team Name* history

9:00 PM – Goal-setting session

10:00 PM – Team snack/downtime

Day 2

7:00 AM – Team workout #3

9:00 AM – Team breakfast

9:30 AM – Classroom

10:30 AM – Final team workout

11:30 AM – Departure

12:15 PM – Team lunch

1:00 PM – Team goal-setting session

AFTER – Player profile pictures/video/interviews

*7:30 PM – Practice

Day 3

    *6:30 PM – Practice

Day 4

    5:00 PM – Team meeting

    6:30 PM – Practice (concludes 7:15 PM)

    7:30 PM – Meet the *Team Name* Event in bar

Day 5

    7:00 PM – HOME vs. Steeldogs (arrive at rink two hours prior)

Day 6

    5:30 PM – AWAY @ Steeldogs (arrive at rink twenty minutes prior to departure)

    *All Practices are one hour unless otherwise noted.

Week 2

Tuesday

    7:00 PM – Team meeting/video session

    8:30 PM – Practice (concludes at 9:15 PM)

Wednesday

    *7:30 PM – Practice

Friday

    *6:30 PM – Practice

    7:45 PM – Team meeting/video session

Saturday

7:00 PM – AWAY @ Lightning (arrive at rink twenty minutes prior to departure)

Sunday

5:30 PM – HOME vs. Lightning (arrive at rink two hours prior)

Week 3

Tuesday

7:00 PM – Team meeting/video session

9:30 PM – Practice (concludes at 10:15)

Wednesday

*7:30 PM – Practice

Friday

*6:30 PM – Practice

7:45 PM – Team meeting/video session

START OF REGULAR SEASON

Saturday

7:30 PM – AWAY @ Steeldogs (arrive at rink twenty minutes prior to departure)

Sunday

5:30 PM – HOME vs. Wildcats (Arrive at rink two hours prior)

For the overnight trip the following items are recommended:

- Three pairs of workout gear
- Multiple pairs of socks
- Warm clothing
- Warm hat
- Towels
- Sleeping gear (sleeping bag, blanket)
- Pillow
- Snacks and drinks

YOU WILL BE ENTERING WATER DURING THIS TRIP

Feel free to contact any member of the coaching staff with questions or concerns.

See you soon!

ACKNOWLEDGMENTS

Just like athletics, the process that goes into writing a book is an endurance test. Moreover, it requires a strong team of family, friends, mentors, and motivators in order to be a success. With that said, there are several people I would like to thank for making *WIN* possible.

First and foremost, I must once again thank my wife and best friend, Janet. I have been blessed by many things in my life. You are by far the one I am most grateful for on a daily basis. None of what I do would matter without your support and love. You have always encouraged me to follow my dreams (even when you aren't completely sure what they are) and you continue to motivate me to grow as a human being. I would be lost in this world without you.

To my children, Logan and Alina. Although you are too young to fully comprehend what Mommy and Daddy do for a living, you serve as the primary motivation source for both of us. There have been many people, events, and situations that have been a catalyst for motivation in our lives. None have come close to creating the drive in us to succeed than you. We love you both with all our hearts.

Mom and Dad, there are not enough words I could write to thank you for your support, guidance, and love throughout my life. Now that I have been a parent for a few years, I am starting to realize how deep a parent's love actually goes. I believe that to be the greatest gift you have both given to me. I will pass it on.

To my brother Alan, his wife, Michelle, and my niece Rachel—watching our families grow together over the past few years has been wonderful. Your love, support, and belief in me, even from afar, inspires me more than you know. I love you all very much.

When the military told my wife and I that we were moving to the UK for three years, we did not know what to expect. I can say, now that we are back in the USA, that our time overseas was nothing short of a blessing. A large part of what made our time so enjoyable was the Peterborough Phantoms organization and their willingness to accept us as part of their family.

ACKNOWLEDGMENTS

Slava Koulikov, head coach of the Peterborough Phantoms and assistant coach of Great Britain's national junior team, I cannot thank you enough for taking a chance on a young American coach, who you barely knew. I had an unorthodox philosophy on how to create a winning team, and your trust in allowing me to implement my team-bonding strategy with our group during your first year with the club is some-thing that I will always be grateful for. I must also thank you and your father for teaching me more about the game and your approach than anyone ever has. I am a better coach because of it. If you had told me years ago that a Russian and American would combine in the sport of hockey to bring a championship to a team in England, I would not have believed it.

James Ferrara, captain of the Peterborough Phantoms— you are what I consider to be the consummate captain. I wrote in this book that coaches must enable their captains as much as captains must enable their coaches. I have not encountered a better example of this than you, during my time coaching. You are a tremendous leader, and seeing the pride on your face when you lifted the playoff trophy for your hometown team is a moment I will cherish forever. Thank you for always being willing to listen and speak when needed. The team is lucky to have you!

Cpl Stu (Staff) Edwards, your approach to leadership and team development is an inspiration to me, our athletes, and the men and women who serve in the Royal Air Force. I am thankful daily that I get to work side by side with you instead of being on the ground doing exercises for you. Thank you for your service to the Phantoms and most importantly to your country!

To the rest of the players who were with the club during my time with the team: When it comes to coaches—you have to hear what we say, but you choose to listen. I want to thank you for choosing to listen and buy into what your coaching staff preached day-in and day-out during the season. At the end of the day, you play the games and deserve all the credit for putting plans into action.

To the owners of the team during my time with the club, Rob and Sue Housden and Dave and Jo Lane, thank you for your willingness to welcome a foreigner to be part of your club. It has been an honor for me to be part of your organization.

Carrie Buckman, I did not have a sister growing up, but if I did, you are what I imagine she would have been like. Your kindness, truthfulness, and guidance (especially when my first child was born) was a gift during a transformative period of my life. I wish you and your family nothing but the best moving forward.

Tom and Diane Scott, your willingness to invite me into your home and talk late into the night (especially about Philadelphia sports) was something that kept me going after many long drives to Peterborough during the season. I am lucky to call you my friends.

ACKNOWLEDGMENTS

Dan Breen, although we were born in different decades, we share so many common interests. I am sure we would have been the best of friends had we gone to school together. I am grateful we have the future to continually "catch up."

Matt Cavalieri, I remember the day we met up in the hospitality section of Planet Ice. Neither of us knew the revolution that was about to begin in Phantoms media at the time, but looking back I am amazed at the things we have accomplished together (including an incredible holiday blooper reel which I watch from time to time for a laugh).

Ian Offers, I hope you are able to find things in this book that will help you as you continue to endeavor into your coaching career. I am just a click away if you ever need me.

Phil Smith, it takes a lot of guts to jump onto a microphone and do play-by-play, having never done it before. One year later and you, along with the media team, have become the gold standard of the EPL broadcasts. I look forward to listening for years to come.

Additional thanks to Jon Kynaston, Jason Buckman, Callum Owen, Rochelle Owen, Dave Tudman, Alan Storer, Shaun Nixon, and the rest of the Phantoms staff. The club's success would not be possible without you.

To the Phantoms' faithful hockey fans, you embody everything that is great about working in pro sports. Your support through thick and thin, while never being afraid to let the boys know what you think of their effort (good or bad), is how fan bases should be. Sharing a championship with you was one of the greatest honors of my life and I hope the Phantoms will provide many more memories like that in the years to come.

I get by with a little help from my friends. I must point out several people who made contributions to this project, either by providing me with information, engaging me in conversation, and/or supporting me as a friend! Jeff Dwyer, hockey goalies are always heralded as being a little crazy— and you absolutely fit the part. Thank you for your friendship and for taking countless hour-plus drives to and from the rink with me during my time in the UK. I honestly don't think I would have survived without that. I look forward to seeing where you go in the future. Tom Moldenhauer— when we moved to England, you were the only person I knew. Thanks to you and your family for always being so warm to ours. I'm glad that for writing this book we were mostly in the same time zone! Stacy Rosales—without your optimism and work ethic none of this would be possible. Can't wait to see what we will do in the future. Alexander Clifford—can't thank you enough for discussing this book with me over several lunches and helping me take a mathematical approach to my theory. Until we meet again! Travis Bowman—you've got heart, kid! Thanks for your help with some of the research in this book. Ray Santiago and Ray Carsillo—my best friends from college—I am privileged to still call you friends after all these years and love that when we speak, it's like no time has passed. Bill, Samantha, and

ACKNOWLEDGMENTS

(my beautiful goddaughter) Nina Weisel—you remain the family I most admire. Thanks for being family to me.

I often credit my undergraduate program at Montclair State University with giving me the tools to be prepared for the professional world. Who knew applying those same tactics to coaching (and teaching) would work just as well! To Dr. Larry Londino, Dr. David Sanders and Patricia Piroh, my professors, advisors, and now friends—I would not have found the success I have in my endeavors without your lessons to me as a young adult. Continue to inspire the young minds of tomorrow!

The ability to accomplish my goals in the sporting world would not have been possible without earning my masters in Sports Management from Drexel University. I want to thank the late David O'Brien, who encouraged me to take writing to the next level, and Dr. Amy Giddings, whose positive nature and ferocious determination made me believe that I could do more in the sporting world than just be an employee. Thank you for encouraging me and inspiring me to follow my heart.

To the creative team at Aloha Publishing—Hannah Cross for your work on getting this started, Jennifer Regner for your proofreading and creative insights, Fusion Creative Works for your designs—thank you for making *WIN* something special.

To Aloha's CEO Maryanna Young—it would be an understatement to say that our work together has changed my life. After two books, I can say that you are one of my favorite people to work with and you continue to inspire me to be better. I am lucky to call you my friend and look forward to working together in the future.

Coaching styles are born from experiences (good and bad) and evolve over time. I want to thank all of my coaches, teachers, and teammates throughout the years for helping me to develop my approach to the game. It would not have been possible without all of you.

Finally, so much of my coaching philosophy is based on the tactics of the military—the humbling difference being that we sacrifice time for a game we love and they sacrifice their lives for a country we love. Some people view comic-book characters and celebrities as superheroes—you continue to serve as mine. Your example of courage and determination have and will always inspire me and countless others. We are indebted to you for protecting our freedom, liberty, and way of life. Thank you all, past, present, and future military service men and women for setting the ultimate example of teamwork.

ABOUT
THE AUTHOR

Lee Elias's credentials are rooted in sports, marketing, and management. He is a graduate of Montclair State University in Upper Montclair, New Jersey, with a BA in broadcasting and an MS degree in sports management from Drexel University in Philadelphia, Pennsylvania. He has built a unique skill set through his professional experience.

He started to coach full time in 2007, at the age of 22, when he was named the general manager and head coach of the Montclair State University Ice Hockey team. During his time with the program, the team saw a dramatic change from the bottom of the league to competing for both regional and national ranking annually.

In 2015, Lee was named as a member of the coaching staff to the Peterborough Phantoms of the English Premier Ice Hockey League (EPIHL), a role he still holds. In his first year with the organization, the team made a dramatic turnaround from being near the bottom of the league during the prior year to winning the league's playoff championship. In addition to coaching, Lee also served as a member of the organization's media team.

Lee is also the founder of Game Seven Group, an organization that works with leaders to help them unlock excellence, reach their potential, and ultimately win using the spirit and culture of a professional sports organization. He is also the co-founder of Sports Achievements and Hockey Wrap Around, both companies that work to make the game of hockey more enjoyable and accessible to the world.

Lee's other sports work experiences include serving the National Hockey League as the Coordinator of the NHL Network during its first season in the USA and working as a camera director for the New York Rangers and New York Knicks at Madison Square Garden. Beyond that, he served as a production specialist with the Pensacola Blue Wahoos (Cincinnati Reds AA) during their inaugural season.

In addition to his sports experience, in 2010 Lee was hired by LocalEdge, a Division of Hearst Media Services. With the company, he helped small-to-medium-sized businesses create digital plans focusing on search engine optimization, search engine marketing, social media marketing, and mobile marketing, among other solutions. Lee also was responsible for development of new consultants and assisting with product development, marketing, product expertise, and public speaking.

Lee is the award-winning author of *Think Like a Fan: Invest in Your Fans So They Invest in You*. Released in 2015, the book covers how organizational leaders can use existing resources to build a culture of fans who are intensely loyal to their brand.

He currently resides in the USA with his wife, Janet, and their two children, Logan and Alina.

Made in the USA
San Bernardino, CA
17 February 2017